"As a man in midlife, I am often reminded that like a piece of fruit or a loaf of bread, I, too, have an expiration date. With this awareness comes searching questions such as, 'What's it all for? Is there meaning to anything that I do, since it will one day all be forgotten? What does it mean to live well in light of such realities?' In characteristic fashion, Os Guinness not only explores these searching questions but offers satisfying, proven answers to them. If you are asking similar questions—or even if you're not—I can't recommend this book to you highly enough."
Scott Sauls, author of *Befriend*

"Most of us feel instinctively that we should seize the day, but is the day worth seizing and should it be grabbed so unreservedly? Os Guinness is a wise and thorough guide to the deep issues surrounding this ancient maxim and helps us gain a clearer perspective on what it means to live life to the fullest."
Steve Turner, journalist, author, and poet

"As an artist, I'm perpetually seeking inspiration to fuel my desire to make a difference in the world. Few thinkers fire me up in that regard more than Os Guinness. *Carpe Diem Redeemed* is no exception."
Max McLean, actor and theater director

"In *Carpe Diem Redeemed*, Os Guinness offers up a splendid reflection on the nature and conception of time and its importance in the self-understanding of a Christian seeking to be faithful in the present era. Guinness calls us to faithful and fearless living, with a sense of humility as we walk before God and endeavor to serve his purposes in our generation."
Trevin Wax, author of *This Is Our Time*

SEIZING THE DAY,
DISCERNING THE TIMES

CARPE
DIEM
REDEEMED

OS GUINNESS

An imprint of InterVarsity Press
Downers Grove, Illinois

InterVarsity Press
P.O. Box 1400, Downers Grove, IL 60515-1426
ivpress.com
email@ivpress.com

InterVarsity Press® is the book-publishing division of InterVarsity Christian Fellowship/ USA®, a movement of students and faculty active on campus at hundreds of universities, colleges, and schools of nursing in the United States of America, and a member movement of the International Fellowship of Evangelical Students. For information about local and regional activities, visit intervarsity.org.

All Scripture quotations, unless otherwise indicated, are taken from the New American Standard Bible®, copyright 1960, 1962, 1963, 1968, 1971, 1972, 1973, 1975, 1977, 1995 by The Lockman Foundation. Used by permission.

While any stories in this book are true, some names and identifying information may have been changed to protect the privacy of individuals.

Published in association with the literary agency of Wolgemuth & Associates.

Chapters 2 and 3 and part of chapter 6 were originally published in Prophetic Untimeliness: A Challenge to the Idol of Relevance *(Baker 2003).*

Cover design and image composite: David Fassett
Interior design: Jeanna Wiggins
Images: diffused color lights © Alexandre Bardol / EyeEm / Getty Images
    sky © John O'neill / EyeEm / Getty Images
    abstract blue wave © oxygen / Moment Collection / Getty Images
    blue watercolor © andipantz / iStock / Getty Images Plus
    rippling water © Olaf Rein / EyeEm / Getty Images
    gold glitter paint © MirageC / Moment Collection / Getty Images
    blue watercolor square © kentarcajuan / E+ / Getty Images
    old fashioned hourglass © mgkaya / E+ / Getty Images

ISBN 978-0-8308-4581-1 (print)
ISBN 978-0-8308-4988-8 (digital)

Printed in the United States of America ♾

Library of Congress Cataloging-in-Publication Data
A catalog record for this book is available from the Library of Congress.

P 24 23 22 21 20 19 18 17 16 15 14 13 12 11 10 9 8 7 6 5 4 3 2 1
Y 39 38 37 36 35 34 33 32 31 30 29 28 27 26 25 24 23 22 21 20 19

DOM

and to CJ,

With love, admiration,

a fierce pride,

and a strong hope

Teach us to number our days,
that we may gain a heart of wisdom.

PSALM 90:12 NIV

There is an appointed time for everything. And there
is a time for every event under heaven—
A time to give birth and a time to die;
A time to plant and a time to uproot what is planted.
A time to kill and a time to heal;
A time to tear down and a time to build up.
A time to weep and a time to laugh.
A time to mourn and a time to dance.
A time to throw stones and a time to gather stones.
A time to embrace and a time to shun embracing.
A time to search and a time to give up as lost;
A time to keep and a time to throw away.
A time to tear apart and a time to sew together;
A time to be silent and a time to speak.
A time to love and a time to hate;
A time for war and a time for peace.

ECCLESIASTES 3:1-8

Time is a created thing. To say "I don't have time,"
is like saying, "I don't want to."

LAO TZU, *TAO TE CHING*

Time was past—thou canst it not recall. Time is thou hast—
employ thy portion small. Time future is not, and may
never be. Time present is the only time for thee.

INSCRIPTION ON AN ANCIENT SUN DIAL

Do not put your work off till tomorrow or the day after,
for a sluggish worker does not fill his barn.

HESIOD, "WORK AND DAYS"

Time will reveal everything. It is a babbler,
and speaks even when not asked.

EURIPIDES

Live for today; plan for tomorrow; remember yesterday.

AESOP

Beware the barrenness of a busy life.

SOCRATES

Heraclitus, I believe, says that all things pass and nothing stays,
and comparing existing things to the flow of a river,
he says you could not step twice into the same river.

PLATO, *CRATYLUS*

Socrates: "There's nothing I like better, Cephalus, than talking with
old men. I see them as travellers who have gone ahead on a
road we too may have to go, and we ought to find out what
it's like—rough and difficult or smooth and easy."

PLATO, *THE REPUBLIC*

As you, so I, so everyone.

ROMAN EPITAPH

Can anything be more ridiculous than a traveller needing
more provisions the closer he is to his destination?

CICERO, "ON OLD AGE"

I will say to my soul, "Soul, you have many goods laid up for many
years to come; take your ease, eat, drink and be merry."
But God said to him, "You fool! This very night your soul is required
of you; and now who will own what you have prepared?"

LUKE 12:19-20

I am convinced that neither death, nor life, nor angels, nor
principalities, nor things present, nor things to come, nor powers, nor
height, nor depth, nor any other created thing, will be able to separate
us from the love of God which is in Christ Jesus our Lord.

ST. PAUL, ROMANS 8:38-39

Be wise, strain the wine and cut back long hope into a small space. Even as we speak, envious time flies past. Seize the day [carpe diem] and leave as little as possible for tomorrow.

HORACE, ODE XI, *FIRST BOOK OF ODES*

There is nothing the busy man is less busy with than living. . . . [The wise man] plans out every day as if it were his last. . . . It is not that we have so little time but that we lose so much. . . . The life we receive is not short but we make it so; we are not ill-provided but use what we have wastefully.

SENECA, *ON THE SHORTNESS OF LIFE*

How trivial life is: yesterday a drop of semen, today a mummy or ashes. Spend therefore these fleeting moments as Nature would have you spend them, and then go to your rest with a good grace, as an olive falls in season, with a blessing for the earth that bore it and a thanksgiving to the tree that gave it life. . . . Perfection of character is this: to live each day as if it were your last, without frenzy, without apathy, without pretense.

MARCUS AURELIUS, *MEDITATIONS*

How can the past and the future be, when the past no longer is, and the future is not yet? As for the present, if it were always present and never moved on to become the past, it would not be time, but eternity.

ST. AUGUSTINE OF HIPPO, *CONFESSIONS*

The wisest are the most annoyed at the loss of time.

DANTE ALIGHIERI, "DIVINE COMEDY"

*Then to the lip of this poor earthen Urn
I leaned, the Secret of my Life to learn:
And Lip to Lip it murmured—"While you live
Drink!—for, once dead, you never shall return."*

OMAR KAYAM, *RUBAIYAT*

There is a tide in the affairs of men, which taken at the
flood leads on to fortune. Omitted, all the voyage of their life is bound
in shallows and miseries. On such a full sea are we now afloat. And
we must take the current when it serves, or lose our ventures.

WILLIAM SHAKESPEARE, *JULIUS CAESAR*

I wasted time, and now doth time waste me.

WILLIAM SHAKESPEARE, *RICHARD II*

Gather ye rosebuds while ye may,
Old Time is still a-flying;
And this same flower that smiles today
Tomorrow will be dying.

ROBERT HERRICK, "TO THE VIRGINS, TO MAKE MUCH OF TIME"

How many things served us yesterday for articles
of faith, which today are fables for us?

MICHEL DE MONTAIGNE, *THE COMPLETE ESSAYS*

Time, like an ever rolling stream, bears all its sons away;
they fly forgotten, as a dream dies at the opening day.

ISAAC WATTS, "O GOD OUR HELP IN AGES PAST"

Every man desires to live long, but no man would be
old. . . . May you live all the days of your life.

JONATHAN SWIFT, *DIALOGUES*

Time is what we want most, but what we use worst.

WILLIAM PENN, LETTER TO
THE LENAPE NATION

You may delay, but time will not.

BENJAMIN FRANKLIN, *POOR RICHARD'S ALMANACK*

Edmund Burke was always right, but he was right too soon.

CHARLES JAMES FOX

Time will explain.

JANE AUSTEN, *PERSUASION*

Write it on your heart that every day is the
best day in the year. No man has learned anything rightly
until he knows that every day is Doomsday.

RALPH WALDO EMERSON, *ESSAYS AND POEMS*

Nothing must be postponed. Take time by the forelock. Now or never!
You must live in the present, launch yourself on every wave, find your
eternity in each moment. Fools stand on their island opportunities and
look toward another land. There is no other land; there is no other life but
this, or the like of this. Where the good husbandman is, there is the good
soil. Take any other course, and life will be a succession of regrets. Let us
see vessels sailing prosperously before the wind, and not simply stranded
barks. There is no world for the penitent and regretful.

HENRY DAVID THOREAU, JOURNAL ENTRY

The cost of a thing is the amount of what I will call life
which is required to be exchanged for it,
immediately or in the long run.

HENRY DAVID THOREAU, *WALDEN*

Life can only be understood backwards, but it has to be lived forwards.

SØREN KIERKEGAARD, *JOURNAL 1843*

My question, the one that brought me to the point of suicide when I was fifty
years old, was a simple one that lies in the soul of every person, from a silly
child to a wise old man. It is the question without which life is impossible,
as I had learnt from experience. It is this: what will become of what I do
today or tomorrow? What will come of my entire life?
Expressed another way the question can be put like this: why do I live?
Why do I wish for anything, or do anything? Or expressed another way: is
there any meaning in my life that will not be annihilated by the inevitability
of death which awaits me?

LEO TOLSTOY, *A CONFESSION*

What if my whole life has really been wrong?

LEO TOLSTOY, *THE DEATH OF IVAN ILYICH*

I can write only from memory. I never write directly
from life. The subject must pass through the sieve of my
memory, so that only what is important . . . remains.

ANTON CHEKHOV, IN RESPONSE TO AN EDITOR

Alice: "How long is forever?"
White Rabbit: "Sometimes just one second."

LEWIS CARROLL, *ALICE IN WONDERLAND*

To know the future is no more desirable in the life of mankind
than in the life of the individual. And our astrological impatience
for such knowledge is sheer folly. . . . A future
known in advance is an absurdity.

JAKOB BURCKHARDT, *REFLECTIONS ON HISTORY*

In his heart every man knows quite well that, being unique, he will
be in the world only once and that there will be no second chance
. . . he knows it but hides it like a bad conscience—why?

FRIEDRICH NIETZSCHE, *UNTIMELY MEDITATIONS*

This life, as you live it at present, and have lived it, you must live it
once more, and also innumerable times; and there will be nothing
new in it, but every pain and every joy and thought and every
sigh, and all the unspeakable small and great in thy life must come
to you again, and all in the same series and sequence.

FRIEDRICH NIETZSCHE, *THE GAY SCIENCE*

Time is a great teacher, but unfortunately it kills all its pupils.

HECTOR BERLIOZ

Time is
Too Slow for those who Wait,
Too Swift for those who Fear,
Too Long for those who Grieve,
Too Short for those who Rejoice,
But for those who Love,
Time is not.

HENRY VAN DYKE, *MUSIC AND OTHER POEMS*

Today will die tomorrow. Time stoops to no man's lure.

CHARLES SWINBURNE, "THE GARDEN OF PROSERPINE"

I am always late on principle, my principle being
that punctuality is the thief of time.

OSCAR WILDE

You have only a few years to live really, perfectly, fully. . . . Time is jealous
of you, and wars against your lilies and roses. You will become sallow, and
hollow-cheeked, and dull-eyed. . . . Live the wonderful life that is in you! Let
nothing be lost upon you. Be always searching new sensations. Be afraid
of nothing. . . . A new Hedonism—that is what our century wants.

OSCAR WILDE, *THE PICTURE OF DORIAN GRAY*

Enjoy life. There's plenty of time to be dead.

HANS CHRISTIAN ANDERSEN, ATTRIBUTED

It is looking at things for a long time that ripens you
and gives you a deeper meaning.

VINCENT VAN GOGH, LETTER TO HIS BROTHER THEO

All men dream: but not equally. Those who dream
by night in the dusty recesses of their minds wake in the day
to find it was vanity: but the dreamers of the day are
dangerous men, for they may act their dreams
with open eyes, to make it possible.

T. E. LAWRENCE, *SEVEN PILLARS OF WISDOM*

Clocks slay time . . . time is dead as long as it is being
clicked off by little wheels; only when the
clock stops does time come to life.

WILLIAM FAULKNER,
THE SOUND AND THE FURY

The past is never dead. It's not even past.

WILLIAM FAULKNER, *REQUIEM FOR A NUN*

The past is a foreign country. They do things differently there.

L. P. HARTLEY, *THE GO-BETWEEN*

Time is evil, a mortal disease, exuding a fatal nostalgia.
The passage of time strikes a man's heart with despair,
and fills his gaze with sadness.

NIKOLAI BERDYAEV, *SOLITUDE AND SOCIETY*

What a wonderful life I've had!
I only wish I'd realized it earlier.

SIDONIE-GABRIELLE COLETTE

The error of the old doctrine of progress
lay in affirming a priori that man
progresses toward the better.

ORTEGA Y GASSET, *HISTORY AS A SYSTEM*

I was, and am, acutely aware that life is ephemeral, limited and brief. I never wake up in the morning without being surprised at being alive: I never go to sleep without wondering whether I shall wake up. Death to me was the reality. Yet everybody I met and saw seemed unaware of it. They seemed to live as if they would live forever. How else could they spend forty years marking exercise-books, going to an office to earn the money which would enable them to go on going to an office which would enable them to go on going to an office—I could see a skull beneath every bowler hat. . . . I was obsessed with the feeling that I was a small boat floating on an ocean, and the ocean was death.

RONALD DUNCAN, *ALL MEN ARE ISLANDS*

Here was a new generation, grown up to find all Gods dead,
all wars fought, all faiths in man shaken.

F. SCOTT FITZGERALD, *THIS SIDE OF PARADISE*

Now he has departed from this strange world a little ahead of me. That means
nothing. People like us, who believe in physics, know that the distinction
between past, present and future is only a stubbornly persistent illusion.

ALBERT EINSTEIN

Being with you and not being with you is the only way I have to measure time.

JORGE LUIS BORGES

There is more to life than simply increasing its speed.

MAHATMA GANDHI

Because things are the way they are,
things will not stay the way they are.

BERTHOLD BRECHT

Real generosity towards the future lies in giving all to the present.

ALBERT CAMUS, *NOTEBOOKS 1935–1942*

There is but one freedom, to put oneself right with death. After that,
everything is possible. I cannot force you to believe in God. Believing in
God amounts to coming to terms with death. When you have accepted
death, the problem of God will be solved—and not the reverse.

ALBERT CAMUS, SCRIBBLED IN THE
MARGINS OF *NOTEBOOKS: 1942–1951*

Time is "an unimportant and superficial characteristic of reality. . . .
To realize the unimportance of time is the gate of wisdom."

BERTRAND RUSSELL, *OUR KNOWLEDGE*
OF THE EXTERNAL WORLD

Do you think that I count the days? There is only one day left, always
starting over; it is given to us at dawn, and taken away from us at dusk.

JEAN-PAUL SARTRE, *THE DEVIL AND THE GOOD LORD*

As often as possible, when a really beautiful bottle of wine is before me,
I drink all I can of it, even when I know I have had more than I want
physically. That is gluttonous. But I think to myself, when again will I have
this taste upon my tongue? Where else in the world is there just such wine
as this, with just this bouquet, at just this heat, in just this crystal cup?
And when again will I be alive to it as I am this very minute, sitting here on
a green hillside above the sea, or in this dim, murmuring, richly odorous
restaurant, or here in this fisherman's café on the wharf?

M. F. K. FISHER, *AN ALPHABET FOR GOURMETS*

To me there is no past or future in art. If a work of art cannot live always
in the present it must not be considered at all. The art of the Greeks, of
the Egyptians, of the great painters who lived in other times, is not an
art of the past, perhaps it is more alive today than it ever was.

PABLO PICASSO

The word death is not pronounced in New York, in
Paris, in London, because it burns the lips.

OCTAVIO PAZ, POET, 1950s

I believe that the reformation of our civilization
must begin with a reflection on time.

OCTAVIO PAZ, *IN LIGHT OF INDIA*

"I wish it need not have happened in my time," said Frodo.
"So do I," said Gandalf, "and so do all who live to see such
times. But that is not for them to decide. All we have to
decide is what to do with the time that is given us."

J. R. R. TOLKIEN, *FELLOWSHIP OF THE RING*

The future is something that everyone reaches at the rate of
sixty minutes an hour, whatever he does, whoever he is.

C. S. LEWIS, *THE SCREWTAPE LETTERS*

Every record has been destroyed or falsified, every book rewritten, every picture has been repainted, every statue and street building has been renamed, every date has been altered. And the process is continuing day by day and minute by minute. History has stopped. Nothing exists except an endless present in which the Party is always right.

GEORGE ORWELL, *1984*

Live as if you were living already for the second time and as if you had acted the first time as wrongly as you are about to act now.

VIKTOR FRANKL, *MAN'S SEARCH FOR MEANING*

There is never time in the future in which we will work out our salvation. The challenge is in the moment, the time is always now.

JAMES BALDWIN, *NOBODY KNOWS MY NAME*

A special consciousness is required to recognize the ultimate significance of time. We all live in it and are so close to being identical with it that we fail to notice it. The world of space surrounds our existence. It is but a part of living, the rest is time. Things are the shore, the voyage is in time.

RABBI ABRAHAM JOSHUA HESCHEL, *THE SABBATH*

It is the time you have wasted for your rose that makes your rose so important.

ANTOINE DE SAINT-EXUPÉRY, *THE LITTLE PRINCE*

The self which seeks the realization of itself within itself destroys itself.

REINHOLD NIEBUHR, *FAITH AND HISTORY*

The past is no good to us. The future is full of anxiety. Only the present is real— the here and now. Seize the day. . . . Grasp the hour, the moment, the instant.

SAUL BELLOW, *SEIZE THE DAY*

How did it get so late so soon? It's night before it's afternoon. December is here before it's June. My goodness, how the time has flewn. How did it get to be so late so soon?

DR. SEUSS

*The function of science fiction is not to
describe the future, but to prevent it.*

RAY BRADBURY, COMMENTING ON ORWELL'S *1984*

*It's paradoxical that the idea of living a long life
appeals to everyone, but the idea of getting
old doesn't appeal to anyone.*

ANDY ROONEY

*One cannot and must not try to erase the past merely
because it does not fit the present.*

GOLDA MEIR, *MY LIFE*

Suspect each moment, for it is a thief, tiptoeing away with more than it brings.

JOHN UPDIKE, *A MONTH OF SUNDAYS*

We are all historians by nature, while we are only scientists by choice.

JOHN LUKACS, *REMEMBERED PAST*

*The saddest aspect of life right now is that science gathers
knowledge more than society gathers wisdom.*

ISAAC ASIMOV

Here we are, trapped in the amber of the moment. There is no why.

KURT VONNEGUT JR., *SLAUGHTERHOUSE-FIVE*

*All photographs are memento mori. To take a photograph is to partake in another
person's (or thing's) mortality, vulnerability, mutability. Precisely by slicing out
his moment and freezing it, all photographs testify to time's relentless melt.*

SUSAN SONTAG, *ON PHOTOGRAPHY*

*I think you can reach a state of consciousness, a state where you are
not aware of anything . . . you're just being. The happiest people are
those who are being more times a week than anybody else.*

JOHN LENNON, INTERVIEW, 1969

Until you value yourself, you won't value your time. Until you value your time, you will not do anything with it.

SCOTT PECK, *A ROAD LESS TRAVELED*

Yesterday has gone. Tomorrow has not yet come. We have only today. Let us begin.

MOTHER TERESA, ATTRIBUTED

The older we get, the better we used to be.

JOHN McENROE

We're brought up to the clock, we're brought up to respect the clock, admire the clock. We live our life to the clock. You clock in to the clock. You clock out to the clock. You come home to the clock. You eat to the clock, you drink to the clock, you go to bed to the clock . . . you do that for forty years of your life, you retire, and what do they give you? An f-ing clock!

DAVE ALLEN, IRISH COMEDIAN

You can live to be 100 if you give up all the things that make you want to live to be 100.

WOODY ALLEN

What can life be worth if the first rehearsal for life is life itself? . . . If we only have one life to live, we might as well not have lived at all.

MILAN KUNDERA, *THE UNBEARABLE LIGHTNESS OF BEING*

The future starts today, not tomorrow.

POPE JOHN PAUL II

Most of Virgin's successes can be attributed to carpe diem moments spurred by optimism.

RICHARD BRANSON, TWEET 2014

It's always about timing. If it's too soon, no one understands. If it's too late, everyone's forgotten.

ANNA WINTOUR, EDITOR OF *VOGUE*

What is more contemptible than a civilization that scorns knowledge of itself?

JOHN RALSTON SAUL,
THE UNCONSCIOUS CIVILIZATION

Today, endless books bang on about "the promotion of successful ageing," largely because the world of technology-and-youth-maddened twenty first century resists the very idea of ageing. Cicero's message was: resist if you must, but much good it will do you. Raging against the dying of the light sounds all very romantic, but it is about as useful as raging against gravity.

PETER JONES, *MEMENTO MORI*

CONTENTS

INTRODUCTION

You Only Live Once—If Then

I HAVE OFTEN TOLD THE STORY of the time I was returning from Brussels to London on the Eurostar. As the train approached St. Pancras Station in central London, it went past some dilapidated Victorian buildings beside the track. Many of them were covered with a splattered mess of graffiti, slogans, and protest symbols. But one wall carried a message that was clearly readable as the train slowed before entering the station.

> You only live once, and it doesn't last.
> So live it up. Drink it down.
> Laugh it off. Burn it at both ends.
> You can't take it with you. You only live once.

Those words are of course a summary of the short-lived YOLO philosophy ("You Only Live Once"). The idea swept many university and college campuses briefly as a much-popularized version of what was taken to be Epicurus's famous maxim, "Eat, drink, and be merry, for tomorrow we die." But regardless of the distortion of Epicurus, it's probable that few devotees of YOLO were aware of one original formulation that set out the philosophy with a sharp sting in its tail: "You only live once—*if then.*"

That blunt version of the YOLO philosophy, and indeed the entire craze for purpose today—books, seminars, conferences, life coaches, slogans, and all—raises important questions: What does it say of how we see the meaning of life, and how we are to make the most of it? From our dawning consciousness of the world as infants to our waking every morning to a new day of life and a world outside us that we can see, hear, and touch, we are always and only at the very center of our lives and therefore at the center of existence as we know it. It is therefore a jolt, a fundamental jolt, to realize how that perspective carries an illusion.

We are simply not at the center of existence. We will not always be here, and the universe will go on without us as if we had never been here. Most people never hear of us even while we are here, and all too soon it will be as if we had never been here at all. For almost all but the tiniest handful of us, the day will come when there is no trace of us in the living memory of the earth.

Thus for all our sense of significance, whether modest or inflated, we are all, as the Greeks said, "mortals." In the words of a Roman epitaph, "As I, so you, so everyone." Or as the Bible states simply, "You are dust, and to dust you will return" (Gen 3:19). Human life is hemmed in by three words and the reality they speak of: *mortality, brevity, fragility*—the last because all that shows we are alive and separates us from death is a mere breath, and one day a single breath will be our last. Who, if they have ever seen a great performance of Shakespeare's *King Lear*, can ever forget the anguish of the old king holding his dead daughter Cordelia in his arms, as if he could put a mirror to her lips and see if there was even the slightest vapor on the glass? "Why should a dog, a horse, a rat have life, and thou no breath at all?"[1]

One single breath? And a finite number of breaths that in a finite number of days could all be counted? Does the shortness of it all leave you dizzy? Does the truth that we are "born to live to die" give life the sense of Milan Kundera's "unbearable lightness of being"? Are we to conclude with the writer of Ecclesiastes, "Vanity of vanities! All is vanity" (Eccles 1:2)? Life is so short, and it can as easily be wasted as lived to the full, so what does it all add up to? How do we make the most of such fleeting days on earth? What does such a *microsecond life* say of our understanding of life, meaning, purpose, identity, truth, and of notions such as right and wrong? What does it say of how we understand what lies behind all of these things—our views of the universe and of time, history, reality, and whether there is a God, gods, or nothing behind it all? And what does it say of how we are to understand the ideal of an "examined life," a "life worth living," and how we live well in our brief stay on earth?

If, as people commonly say today, our brief lives are simply "the dash between the two dates on our gravestones," what hope is there of investing that brief dash with significance? There are truths that no one can answer for us. We must each face them alone. Our own mortality is one of them. How challenging to stand and ask as Tolstoy asked himself, "What will come of my entire life? . . . Is there any meaning in my life that will not be annihilated by the inevitability of death which awaits me?"[2] And how terrible to come close to the end of life and have to say with Tolstoy's Ivan Ilyich, "What if my whole life has been wrong?"[3]

In short, our human challenge is to make the most of our time on earth and to know how to do it. Time and space are the warp and woof of the reality in which we live our brief lives as humans, but they are different. When Alexander the Great asked Diogenes if there was anything he could do for him, the flinty old philosopher answered famously, "Stand out of my light!" We can occupy part of space exclusively and block someone else's access, but no one occupies time exclusively. Time is our "commons," the open and shared ground for all who are alive at any moment to enjoy together.

More importantly, we humans can conquer space, and we do so easily and routinely with our bulldozers, our cranes, our smart phones, our jets, and all the shiny achievements of our technological civilization. But we cannot conquer time. Time does not lie still before us like space, for it is within us as well as around us, and it is never stationary. It moves, and in one direction only—onwards and unstoppable. In the words of Abraham Joshua Heschel, philosopher and rabbi, "Man transcends space, and time transcends man."[4]

Importantly too, the comparative ease of our conquest of the world of physical space disguises a vital fact: our conquests of space are always at the expense of using up time. We are spending our time even if we twiddle our thumbs and do nothing, and energetic activism does not solve the problem. We can build "bigger and bigger barns" or bigger and bigger empires, whether political or commercial, but there is always a day or a night when life ends, and then, as Jesus of Nazareth warned, "your soul is required of you" (Lk 12:20). Which means that the time we have spent in doing anything is the real cost and the proper key to assessing whether we have gained or lost and the effort has been worthwhile. However effortless-seeming our accomplishments, we always pay for them at the expense of our greatest challenge and the most insoluble mystery of our lives—time. "What does it profit a man," Jesus also declared, "to gain the whole world, and forfeit his soul?" (Mk 8:36).

Look around the world today at all our high-striding billionaires, multibillionaires, and soon-to-be trillionaires. They may be titans of finance or technology or political power, but face-to-face with time they are the same little people, the same mortals we all are. Whatever their plans and their dreams for the future, whatever their intentions and their resolutions, whatever their energy and their resources, death waits for them at the end as for us all, and death is therefore truly humanity's "final enemy," whatever the hopes of the life-extension dreamers. Heroes or villains, saints or sinners, world-famous or unknown, we all die in the end. All human life is time bound: it always has been, and it always will be. Our basic condition is what the novelist and poet Thomas Hardy called "time-torn."[5]

Yet the challenge of time is sharper still for us as modern people. Karl Marx famously described workers in the Industrial Revolution as "wage slaves," and quite apart from the thought of death at the end of life, many of us in our advanced modern world know well that we are as much "time slaves" as some are "wage slaves" and "debt slaves." Life in the instant world of advanced modernity is fired at us point blank. And since we are encouraged to realize that life will speed up further as things are made even more "efficient," does it mean that we are living too slowly and inefficiently now? We have less control over our time than ever, which is the real index of slavery. We are under the gun as never before—running, running, running and never catching up. (Most of us, we are told, are "triple screen-gazers" and check our smart phones more than one hundred times a day, which is only one aspect of our constant state of partial attention and always feeling behind.)

Yet for all our frustrations and complaints about the "rat race," we often do not give much thought to all that lies behind it and

how we can begin to counter it. Which means we are all the more
vulnerable to the efficiency experts and to new fashions that turn
out to be false answers, and to some that make the problem even
worse. And there is always the thought that we do not want to
admit: If our own technologies have made us into time slaves, we
have done it to ourselves.

How then are we to think about the challenge of time today,
and how are we to live more freely under the pressures of modern
fast life? There is no escape from being time bound and time torn,
for that is part and parcel of our being human. But is there an
answer to the nightmare of time slavery in the here and now, and
therefore to seeing time well and making the most of life?

"JUST DO IT" TO "JUST BUY IT"

Philosopher Roman Krznaric's bestselling *Carpe Diem Regained*
captures the modern dilemma superbly, and my own title is a
deliberate variation on his.[6] He has set out to explore the present
status of the famous two-word maxim *carpe diem*, "seize the day,"
from the Roman poet Horace's celebrated Ode 11. As Krznaric sees
it, the motto has never been more popular, and it is now inter-
preted variously as a matter of five main approaches to time:
grasping an opportunity, going for pleasure, practicing presence,
developing spontaneity, and pursuing a certain style of politics.
The distinguished English actor Judi Dench had the motto tat-
tooed on her wrist on her eighty-first birthday, and Hollywood
captured the philosophy brilliantly in the film *Dead Poets Society*.
Robin Williams played a teacher in a New England school, urging
his students in poetry class: "We are food for worms, lads. Because, believe it or not, each and every one of us in this room is
going to stop breathing, grow old and die. . . . [Therefore] Carpe
diem. Seize the day, boys. Make your lives extraordinary."[7]

At the same time, Krznaric argues, the passionate desire to not miss out on life has been pulled off course by a welter of current distortions and look-alikes. Seizing the day, making the most of the moment, and living each moment to the fullest has been hijacked and redirected to such false ends as consumerism, hedonism, workaholism, mindfulness, and irresponsibility. Nike's "Just do it," he says, has morphed into "Just buy it," "Just plan it," and "Just watch it."

Krznaric's book is a fascinating tour of the contemporary horizon concerning responses to time in the modern world. It shines a searching light on all sorts of current follies and pitfalls in handling time and therefore on the challenge of living a "good life" and an "examined life" today. Yet with the selective attention typical of so many of today's thinkers, his own answer overlooks the perspective of the most radical view of time that once shaped the Western world and that shines out today like a lighthouse in the storm that is advanced modern life—the unique perspective of the Hebrew and Christian Scriptures. He admits that his omission is deliberate and his short-sightedness is self-induced. "I don't believe there is any ultimate meaning of life, whether written in scripture, the stars or our DNA. If it is meaning we seek, we can—and must—create it for ourselves."[8]

Create it for ourselves? Like Bertrand Russell, with the great English philosopher's view of the Greek giant Atlas who carried his own world on his own shoulders, Krznaric does not believe there is any meaning of life that is "inherent" in the universe or "out there," to be discovered. If anyone desires meaning today, they will have to create it by themselves and carry it by themselves. Nothing else is conceivable. By definition, the atheists' or agnostics' search for the meaning of time and life can never amount to more than a Do-it-Yourself endeavor.

The truth is that the DIY secularist view of time is a major and widely regarded answer, but it is only one answer among the world's many answers and a minority answer at that. Yet when it comes to a challenge as profound as time, all answers should be considered and none should merely be asserted as if self-evident or taken on trust simply because the speaker is an eminent philosopher or a bestselling author. As always, contrast is the mother of clarity, and the differences between the answers make a difference—and make a difference not only for individuals but for whole societies and civilizations.

This book sets out the contours of the very different answer that Krznaric overlooks—the Bible's. Unfortunately, this Jewish and Christian perspective came to be blindly accepted in the West with too few questions asked, and it is now blindly rejected in the West with too few questions asked. Over against the earlier attitude, I am not asking for any special treatment, and over against the current attitude, all I would seek is a fair hearing for a view that is distinctive, radical, and magnificently consequential for each of us as individuals as well as for the future of humanity. For surely it is undeniable that a wise understanding and a positive response to time and history is as vital to the future of humanity as it is to each one of us in our daily lives.

Carpe diem, "seize the day," or make the most of life is a magnificent ideal, but how are we to achieve it? How are we to make it more than a slogan and a cliché fit only for a college student's poster? How are we to take it beyond its three most obvious pitfalls, seizing the day in a selfish or a short-term manner, or cultivating a style of spontaneity that is only a silly form of randomness? And how are we to do it under the unrelenting pressures of modern fast life? Science, by its very nature, can give us explanations for things, but it cannot provide the meaning we are asking for. Philosophy, after three thousand years, has sharpened our thinking, but it has brought us little nearer to solid answers. For all the skepticism of today, and the refusal to think too deeply, the wisdom of the ages still holds true that we must look to ultimate beliefs.

My argument here is simple, straightforward, and a sure way forward. Seizing the day and making the most of life must not be flaunted in the face of impossibility or absurdity; the ideal requires a vision of life capable of fulfilling it. And that, I will argue, can best be found within an ultimate belief, a faith, a relationship, a trust that does justice to the deepest meaning of time, of history, and of human significance and enterprise.

In short, seizing the day, making the most of life, and understanding the meaning of life are inseparable. All three require that if we are to master time, we must come to know the author of time, the meaning of time, and come to know the part he calls us to play in his grand story, which makes the deepest overall sense of time and history. Even more, wonder of wonders, we are then invited to live lives that align our individual hopes and destinies with the very purpose and destiny of the universe itself.

SINGULAR, SIGNIFICANT, AND SPECIAL

THERE IS AN OLD CHINESE PROVERB, "If you want to know what water is, the fish is the last thing to ask." Rudyard Kipling wrote similarly in his poem "The English Flag," "And what should they know of England who only England know?" Those two sayings turn on a common fact that also makes the challenge of time such a mystery to us as humans. Fish that can only live in water will never be able to understand the water that is their sole environment, and the English in Kipling's generation who had never been abroad were incapable of understanding their empire and were blind to the worst of its consequences.

In the same way, we humans are so immersed in time that we will never be able to see and understand time objectively. Time is at the heart of existence. Time is the all-embracing medium of our lives, within us as well as around us, which means that we have no counter environment from which to look at time with detachment and perspective. Indeed, along with evil, time is one of the greatest mysteries in human life—evil being impenetrable through its darkness, and time being mysterious to us because of its closeness. What time is may seem obvious—obvious, that is, until we are asked to explain it. St. Augustine put it memorably: "What then is time? If no one ask of me, I know; if I wish to explain to him who asks, I know not."[1]

What was there before the beginning of time and the beginning of the world? What will it be like when "time shall be no more"? What might it be like to be outside of time? If we have to answer such questions by ourselves, there is simply no way to know or to say. Theoretical physicist Stephen Hawking once remarked that such questions are like standing at the South Pole and asking which way is south. We are in time, and time is in us, so questions about what time is and what is beyond time are unanswerable from our vantage point alone.

If you are completely baffled by the mystery of time, you are not alone. An eminent twentieth-century physicist put forward a profound-sounding statement, "Time is nature's way to keep everything from happening all at once."[2] But he then admitted in a footnote that the quotation did not come from Albert Einstein, Kurt Gödel, or any philosopher or scientist, but from graffiti in the men's room at a café in Austin, Texas.

In an early entry in his journal, the eminent analytical philosopher Ludwig Wittgenstein noted that the meaning of a system lies outside the system, and his point is true above all of life, the world, and time and history. Their full meaning, if indeed there is such a thing, does not lie within them but must come from outside them. The mystery of time will always be insoluble if considered from within time alone. What helps us make a beginning, however, is that humans have long attempted to understand all they could of time, from within time, and their different pictures illuminate time in contrasting ways. With time, as with almost all of the big questions of life, there are three major families of faiths offering answers—extended families of faiths in the sense that there are common family resemblances, although with differences, between philosophies or faiths that share a common notion of what is ultimately real. Viewed from this vantage point, the three major families of faiths are the Eastern, the Abrahamic, and the secularist, and out of them have grown three dominant and very different views of time and history—the *cyclical*, the *covenantal*, and the *chronological*.

Each extended family of faiths gives a dramatically different answer to the big questions of life, one of them claiming to have a view that comes from outside time, but they all start by facing up to the same existential challenge of time and history. In historian Mircea Eliade's words, we humans are all confronted by the same "terror of history, with its randomness, its contingencies, its apparent meaninglessness."[3] Born into the world, we are each given a short life to live, but nature and the world around us do not by themselves inform us of the rhyme and reason to life. And as we look around, there is no obvious meaning to things as they are. We can see both beauty and brokenness, disasters and serendipities, random acts of cruelty as well as kindness, and always endings, endings, endings.

This too shall pass. Time flies. Nothing lasts forever. You cannot step into the same river twice because the river is different and so too are you. The grandest and most magnificent human endeavors are only sandcastles washed away by time and tide. And our own small enterprises and endeavors appear to be whistling into the winds of history. In the end, the sands of time will cover everything without a trace of who we are and what we have done.

Or so it seems. And if that is so, what is the meaning of it all? Why does anything matter? And how are we to live if we are only here once, and the time we are here is so short?

CYCLICAL TIME

The first major family of faiths responds by concluding that though life is short, we are not here only once. It then sets out an entirely different picture of existence based on that assumption. Its view is that time and history are *cyclical*, that we all experience successive reincarnations, that everything comes back to the place from which it started, and that our only hope for freedom is to *escape from the perplexity of history and the illusion of reality altogether*—into the realm of the changeless beyond this world of flux and change.

This cyclical view starts with observations from nature, and its underlying picture is of time as a wheel. The immediate appeal of this view lies in its reflections on what we all see in the natural world around us. The planets revolve in the heavens, and the seasons of the year come and go. Spring leads to summer, summer to autumn, autumn to winter, and winter to spring once again. In the same way, the clouds come down as rain, the rain washes down to the river, and the river to the sea, and the sea evaporates in its turn to form clouds, which once more come down as rain, and so the cycle continues endlessly. Aristotle summed up the cyclical view as the classical Greeks understood it, "Coming to be and passing away, as we have said, will always be continuous and will never fail."[4]

On one level, we humans seem to fit this cyclical picture in that we too are subject to the processes of nature. Like all animals, we go through a succession of seasons or passages in our lives. We wake and we sleep. We are born, we grow, we decline, and we die.

The classical authors described these *age stages* differently. Generally, there were three (youth, maturity, and old age), but Pythagoras and Horace divided them into four, Hippocrates into seven, and Solon into ten. The most famous description in English is William Shakespeare's immortal seven ages of man: "At first the infant, mewling and pewking in his mother's arms" moving through five more seasons of life to the "Last scene of all, that ends this strange eventful history, is second childishness and mere oblivion, sans teeth, sans eyes, sans taste, sans everything."[5]

Shakespeare, of course, wrote from within the second family of faiths, not the first. He did not believe that the entire universe moved in cyclical time. Today the two main proponents of the grand cyclical view of time are the Hindus and the Buddhists, but in the ancient world there were many who held this view. Buddhism is in essence a reform movement of Hinduism, so there are important differences between the two views and their ways of life, just as there are many differing traditions within each religion. But they share the overall view of the radically cyclical view of time. Indeed, they go beyond the evidence of the cycle that lies before our five senses and project the notion of the cycle onto the very cosmos itself in the form of reincarnation. Everything goes around and around, and then returns to where it began, as a matter of what the Eastern religions call "reincarnation" and Friedrich Nietzsche called "eternal recurrence."

Seen this way, time is an ever-moving wheel. Human life in time is life bound to this wheel, as desire leads to craving, which leads to attachment, which leads to death, which leads to reincarnation, and so it goes. Ethics, then, is a matter of *karma* and a question of what each of us has done in some previous incarnation. History, like a wheel spinning in place, goes nowhere, and freedom (*moksha*, "release" or salvation) can be achieved only as an escape from the wheel and so from history and the world that we take to be real but is in fact only an illusion (*maya*). Importantly, there is no way to stop the cycle from within the cycle, so the only way to be free is to escape the cycle itself—by adopting one of the recommended paths to salvation, such as yoga for the Hindus and "right mindfulness" for the Buddhists.

Unquestionably, the cyclical view of time does justice to an enormous part of our experience of life and to many of the operations of nature that we can observe. Recognizing that part is vital to realism and wisdom, but at what price do we make it the whole story of life? Does the cyclical view do justice to the whole reality of human existence and provide an adequate answer to the significance of humans and the challenge of time? And what are the consequences of holding this view? If everything goes around and around and around, and always returns to where it began, is there any escape from the oppressive weightiness of remorseless *karma*, fate, and destiny? And if everything goes around and around and comes back to where it started, what does that say of our actions in history, especially if history and the world that we know are only an illusion? ("What history relates," Arthur Schopenhauer wrote, "is in fact only the long, heavy and confused dream of mankind.")[6]

Why is there a striking absence of any call to "change," to "reform," or to work for something that is truly new? Why is there so little of the "novel" and the "revolutionary" within the cyclical view? If all that is once was and will be all over again, how do we escape such a natural reinforcement of passivity and the status quo? If everything is ultimately unchanging, is it also unchangeable? Do our actions have significance here and now, or—as a Zen saying expresses it—are humans only as "a stone thrown in the pond, who causes no ripples"?

COVENANTAL TIME

Today, the cyclical view of time is mainly associated with Eastern religions. Many people think it must be a minority view because it differs from the mainstream modern view that has shaped the West, but from the vantage point of history that conclusion is seriously skewed. The cyclical view was nearly universal in many periods of history, and it is likely to emerge strongly again if the views that succeeded and eclipsed it falter in their turn—witness, for example, Nietzsche's rejection of God and his turn towards "eternal recurrence." In other words, many people in the West take their view of time and history for granted and do not realize how radically unique it was when first it burst upon the world through the Bible and the Jewish people.

The Abrahamic family of faiths sees time and history quite differently from the very beginning, at creation, and it has important differences from the purely cyclical view all the way down the line. Crucially, it is the one family of faiths that does not claim to be an understanding of the system from *within* the system—and therefore qualifies at once to be assessed in light of Wittgenstein's claim that the true meaning of the system must come from outside the system. In contrast to the Eastern views (and as we saw with Bertrand Russell and Roman Krznaric, all later secularist views too), the Abrahamic view claims to be the result of *revelation* rather than reflection, a matter of *divine disclosure from the outside* rather than discovery through the quest of some religious genius such as Siddhartha Gautama or Shankaracharya. And the differences proliferate from there.

According to the Hebrew and Christian Scriptures, and in strong contrast to the surrounding cultures of Babylon and Egypt as well as the Eastern religions, time and history are viewed not

only as cyclical but as *linear and covenantal.* The truth behind this
truth is the sovereign freedom of God and the fact that human
beings, created in the image and likeness of God, are also free.
They are free with a freedom that is unfathomable but precious
and unique among the life forms on the earth. Many implications
flow from this foundational idea of created freedom, but at their
core is a titanic truth and a momentous message that completely
transforms the meaning of life: *Time and history have meaning.
Under the twin truths of God's sovereignty and human significance,
time and history are going somewhere, and each of us is not only
unique and significant in ourselves, but we have a unique and significant part to play in our own lives, in our own generation, and
therefore in the overall sweep of history.*

One might stop right there and ponder the marvel of that truth.
Once again, contrast is the mother of clarity. Time and history are
not an illusion or *maya,* as Hinduism and Buddhism see it. They
are not meaningless or, as Shakespeare's Macbeth put it, "a tale,
told by an idiot, full of sound and fury, signifying nothing."[7] We
are not dust blowing in the wind. We are not a freak accident lost
in a universe that came to be without meaning and one day will
cease to be without meaning. Paul Johnson captured the stunning
contribution of this Hebrew view in the opening pages of his *A
History of the Jews*: "No people has ever insisted more firmly than
the Jews that history has a purpose and humanity a destiny. . . .
The Jewish vision became the prototype for many similar grand
designs for humanity, both divine and man-made. The Jews,
therefore, stand right at the center of the perennial attempt to
give human life the dignity of a purpose."[8]

The result is an immense and magnificent transformation.
What Mircea Eliade called the "terror of history," history viewed

as random and meaningless, is transformed into the "task of history," filled with significance and meaning. What the Eastern religions advocate as a freedom that is an "escape from history" becomes, within the biblical view, a freedom and responsibility that is an "engagement with history," and a commitment to work for freedom, justice, and shalom in this life and in this world.

In the Bible's view, this radically different view of time, history, and human freedom goes back to the radically different understanding of God and the radical difference it makes. God, as we encounter him in the Bible, is completely different from all other conceptions of the gods. God is not a superman or a demigod projected onto the skies by humanity. He is not the personification of any of the forces of nature, such as the sun, the sea, or the storm. He is not another name for the spirit or sum total of the very cosmos itself, as in pantheism, monism, or notions of Being. According to the Bible and the Abrahamic family of faiths, all such notions of God are a false projection and inflation of what is merely a part of the universe and not God at all, and therefore an idol or a nothing.

As God reveals himself in the Bible, he is absolutely unique in two foundational ways. On the one hand, God is transcendent and utterly Other—the One who is "only, outside, and over all" (radical monotheism) and therefore sovereignly free. At the same time, God is personally and passionately engaged with his creation and on behalf of his creation, and especially committed to and concerned for the human creatures he has made in his image and likeness. God loves us and believes in us as humans even more than we love and believe in ourselves.

Together, these two features radically distinguish "the God of Abraham, Isaac, and Jacob" from both "the gods of the ancients" and from what Blaise Pascal, in his famous "night of fire," called the god of "philosophers and scholars."[9] As the creator of the cosmos and everything that is in it, God transcends nature and nature's ways of operating (or laws), and he is not bound by what he has created. As creator of time as well as space, God is outside time. But unlike Aristotle's "prime mover" who is the "unmoved mover" of so much philosophy, or the remote "clockmaker" or absentee "designer god" of deism, God is personal and therefore engaged in history and with humanity. He alone is sovereign and therefore absolutely free to express and execute his will without restraint or interference. Limited only by his character, he is unlimited in his freedom and power to act and to intervene in time and history. "I am who I am," or "I will be who I will be" (Ex 3:14). God speaks and acts solely because he wills to speak and act, sovereignly and freely, but with the mercy and compassion that express who he is. Unmoved mover? No, Rabbi Heschel counters. God is "the most moved mover."[10]

Made "in the image and likeness" of God, we humans are exceptional, responsible, and consequential. We are free and capable of real choice—"I have set before you life and death, the blessing and the curse. So choose life" (Deut 30:19). Being free, we could always do otherwise than we have chosen and done, so we are responsible for what we have chosen and done. We are therefore significant and responsible, though we are not sovereign as God is, and we are always limited by our finiteness and by our proneness to corrupt freedom and so to go wrong, do wrong, and even to become prisoners to our freely chosen wrongdoing. Formed from "the dust of the earth," we are part of nature and nature's laws, and there is definitely a cyclical element to our lives—we too experience the seasons and passages of life, from birth through growth to decline and death.

But made in "the image and likeness" of God, and given "the breath of life" by God, we are exceptional because we are different from the other animals. We have a consciousness that is both self-conscious and thus aware of ourselves ("I am I") and a consciousness too that, aware of the reaches of time, can stand back and view time with a certain perspective—including the remote past, the immediate present, and the distant future.

When it comes to our awareness of time, this human freedom depends crucially on three faculties. Together, they allow us to go beyond the world that is right in front of us and beyond the immediate moment. We can therefore engage the vast reaches of time and history, and to a significant extent gain greater mastery over time than the rest of creation. Animals have time wired into them, as we can observe from the hibernation of animals and the migration of birds, but our human grasp of time is far richer.

First, our awareness of time includes *memory* of the past, which brings the vast expanse of the past to our consciousness and makes the past a living factor in the present. Second, our awareness of time includes *imagination and vision*, which opens up the future to our consciousness, and brings in the future as a living factor in the present. And third, our awareness of time includes *will*, which expresses the freedom of our human agency and allows us to bring our consciousness of the past and the future to bear on the choices by which we act into the present.

TIME AND FREEDOM

These points are worth pondering further. For example, our age is so obsessed with the future and so impatient with the past that we need to remind ourselves of the liberating role of memory. If you think about it, the stories of the remarkable decisions and heroic deeds in the past make history memorable, and they in turn can inspire the present and rescue it from the stifling impression of inevitability. The truth is that well-taught history and well-written biography are both vital to freedom and anything but boring. As we remember the story of Moses, or Francis of Assisi, or Abraham Lincoln, or Florence Nightingale, or Winston Churchill, or Martin Luther King Jr., or Mother Teresa, the past can inspire us to rise above our present moment, just as the heroes of the past rose above the lethargy of their own present and its seemingly ironclad circumstances.

The "dead hand of the present" may be every bit as oppressive as the "dead hand of the past." Some of the forces from the past, such as language, tradition, and law, will always act as powerful shapers of the present, but the memory of the past can also inspire and liberate the present so that inevitability gives way to innovation. In Reinhold Niebuhr's words, "Memory is, in short, the fulcrum of freedom for man in history."[11] Complacency makes the past appear unchallengeable. Haven't things always been this way? But freedom summons up creativity, innovation, change, growth, and discontent, and it challenges the aura of inevitability that the past lays on the present.

Unquestionably, the human will is central to the biblical view of human freedom and responsibility, but for both good and ill, for creation and destruction. According to the Bible, an inclination to evil through the corruption of the will now lies at the heart of human nature and its use and abuse of freedom. Humans can willfully defy God and the structures of their existence, and through their abuse of freedom bring evil into the world. Indeed, far from diminishing as time goes by, as the progressives fondly believe, this willful defiance will rise to a crescendo at the end of days in the person of the Antichrist. At times, this evil can be so potent that it can be countered only by the backstop of God's providence. Thus "under God" is no cliché. Providence is the ultimate check and balance, the final moral limit to human power.

Without a doubt, this insistence on the open-ended potential of human freedom is sobering—the freedom that is the source of sublime creativity (in a Michelangelo statue, a Shakespeare sonnet, or a Mozart concerto) is the very source of destructive power that destroys other humans (in designing and running a death camp) and could one day be the ruin of the planet. Such an open-ended view of freedom is enlightening and encouraging, but mention of the freedom at the heart of evil is also offensive and sobering. Pascal noted in *Pensées* that "Nothing offends us more rudely than this doctrine; and yet, without this mystery, the most incomprehensible of all, we are incomprehensible to ourselves."[12]

Alongside the open and willful defiance of God, it is also true that people can drift and slowly lose their freedom without realizing it. Almost imperceptibly they can bow before other people and their opinions; before outside forces such as drugs, alcohol, and pornography; or slide into slavery before the accumulated power of their own bad choices (the "habits of the heart" in a negative form). They then become children, slaves, or addicts, and they are no longer free. In the biblical view, the end of the line for both willful wrongdoing and the slow self-enslavement through bad choices and bad habits is the "hardened heart," the condition through which once-free people lose their independence and become the prisoners of their own stubbornly proud but wrong choices.

Together, the triple impact of memory, imagination, and will enlarges what we mean by the present. Far from a fleeting nanosecond that has gone almost as soon as it arrives, the present is a moment rich with the meaning of the past and the meaning of the future and their combined potential for meaningful action in the present.

Thus, under this very different understanding of God, the Bible opens up a view of time and history that is not only cyclical but linear and covenantal. Emphatically, the biblical view is neither purely cyclical nor ultimately cyclical. Humans are certainly part of nature, and the cyclical element is obvious and inescapable. But created in the image and likeness of God, we humans are free, active, responsible, creative, innovative, and consequential. We have a unique agency in the world around us, and we are called to a unique task: partnership with God on behalf of his world, which is what makes time not only linear but covenantal. We are both created and creative. We humans have both the freedom and the responsibility to live and to act into time and into history.

Along with all life and along with the cosmos itself, we humans are created. But uniquely we are not only created but creative. We have the freedom and responsibility to live and to act into time and history, and to bring into being what has not yet been. Above all, our creativity is the creativity to create ourselves— through the myriad of choices that form the habits of the heart that form the people we become. Freedom, as C. S. Lewis argued in *The Great Divorce*, is the gift by which we humans most resemble our Maker. Freedom is therefore the grand assumption of human history, just as history—both for better and for worse—is the grand demonstration of human freedom.

We must never allow words such as *freedom* to become civic or pious clichés. The stakes are too high to treat freedom casually. *The Bible's view of humanity is the highest and most balanced humanism in all history, and the implications for freedom and responsibility are momentous.* Humans are exceptional among all the forms of life on earth: created to be both free and responsible, we are exceptional in that we alone can exercise our memory, our vision, and our will to make choices that make a decisive difference for good or ill, for order or for chaos, for justice or injustice in our planet home. Countless millennia after creation, we humans are still exceptional, we still have choices, and our choices still have consequences—now more consequential than ever. To a large extent we humans become what we choose, and to that extent we are in part, but only in part, self-created (or self-ruined).

THE DIFFERENCE THAT MAKES A DIFFERENCE

Many important points follow from this understanding of freedom. But the basic implication is revolutionary: *the past influences but does not close the circle in determining the future, so freedom means that the future may always be different from the past.* There is no fate, inevitability, necessity, or historical determinism in the Bible's view of history. There is no Nietzschean "eternal recurrence" or any cosmic equivalent of Yogi Berra's "déjà vu all over again." Freedom means that real choice, real creativity, and therefore real change and real innovation are always possible. We can learn from our experiences and decide to do differently the next time. Things can always be otherwise. What will be can be different from what was. We can change social and political circumstances that appear massive and immovable, but far more importantly, we ourselves can change. We can be other than we were or other than we are. Real change, real reform, real growth, and real development are all possible, as freedom gives them a potential that is unimaginable.

The Bible's view of human freedom is completely different from all the numerous forms of determinism, whether ancient or modern, and many simple but revolutionary truths follow from this basic truth. First, freedom requires humility and defies the arrogance of

rationalist certainty. Our human freedom is always and ultimately
mysterious and partially unpredictable, even when it comes to ourselves, and more so when it comes to others. No one knows exactly
why other people are acting and how they will act and therefore
what the next moment will bring when they act freely. The future
will always contain suspense, surprise, and shock. Absolutely no
one—not the most confident pundit; the wisest, most experienced,
and highest paid consultant; or the best data-driven analyst—will
ever be able to close the circle and tell us with certainty all that will
happen next in history. Freedom demands humility, and the intellectual arrogance that is a key feature of the modern managerial
elites is a fatal handicap for enduring freedom.

Second, freedom is truly creative in relation to the future.
Freedom and choice mean that history is the arena for creativity
and change, and humans can be the agents of protest, innovation,
transformation, growth, renewal, and reform. Like freedom itself,
the notion of reform is surrounded with confusion and contro-
versies today because of the massive differences between revolutions inspired by the Bible (such as the English, 1642, and the
American, 1776) and revolutions inspired by the French Enlightenment (such as the French, 1789, the Russian, 1917, and the
Chinese, 1949). The roots of constructive reform lie in the vision
and truths of the Bible. God calls Abraham to break with the gods
and practices, the worship and ways of life of the surrounding
nations, which in turn becomes an ongoing protest against all that
distorts the understanding of God and all that dehumanizes the
treatment of persons made in his image and likeness. The result
is the calling of prophets as social critics who address wrongs and
promote justice. The result is a commitment to creativity, change,
renewal, and reform that repairs humanity and keeps alive the
human dream of freedom, justice, and peace.

Dead religion has all too often become the mainstay of the status quo and of oppression, but a living faith in God is the automatic refusal to accept the world as it is and a restless quest to make it what it should be under God and one day will be again. There is no dropping out, no settling back, and no withdrawing in the life of faith. Faith is a lifetime commitment to an ongoing journey toward the renewal and restoration of the world.

Third, freedom is potentially redemptive in relation to the past. If freedom means genuine choice, then not only can the future be different, so also can the past be different in a significant way. Thus wrongdoing in the past need not have the inevitably disastrous consequences it would have otherwise. This point is profoundly important today, when we are seeing a widening chasm between the Bible's way of righting wrong and many current ways, such as that of postmodern and power-driven, left-wing progressivism. Not long ago, Stalinists on the left and McCarthyites on the right both used the malignant tactic of destruction through accusation. But now we have what *New York Times* columnist David Brooks calls "the cruelty of call-out culture." Instant social media mobs destroy people at the mere unearthing of a sin from the past or the slightest accusation of any sin in the present—with no right to a hearing, no sense of context, no checking of the facts, and no allowance for change and growth, let alone repentance and forgiveness. The result is "a vengeful game of moral one-upmanship in which social annihilation can come any second."[13]

Jews and Christians are no less realistic about the evil of past evils. But in the biblical view, human freedom means the past can be significantly changed, even after blatant wrongdoing. For, quite apart from God's intervention in time, there is always the double possibility of an evildoer's decision to repent and be sorry, and a victim's decision to forgive rather than retaliate. When either or both of these human responses happen, and both are the fruit of freedom as well as grace, they short-circuit the natural course of dark responses and open up a brighter future.

That is the freedom expressed in the second half of Oscar Wilde's famous saying, "Every saint has a past and every sinner has a future." It is also what makes it both realistic and constructive to "hate the sin, but not the sinner." The sin is always and forever wrong—in the past, the present, and the future. But the "sinner" need not be stuck in the past, for there is a difference between the act and the person who did the act. Repentant, forgiven, and transformed, yesterday's sinner may be freed from the past to become tomorrow's saint. In strong contrast to the secular view, no past is irredeemable in the biblical view, which is a vital step in the overall task of "redeeming the time" and growing through the whole course of life.

Fourth, freedom always necessitates living with risk and insecurity. This is an inescapable implication of covenantal time and history: the human story will always be open-ended. It may go one way or another way. By its very nature, freedom can never be finally and ultimately secure and permanent. Trust, risk, daring, and insecurity are all part of the price of freedom, and any attempt to create false security and an illusion of permanence will be a sure road to killing freedom. The United States and the West are learning this old lesson again, but it is an enduring lesson of history. However strong or free individuals or nations may be, whether Egypt, Babylon, Persia, Greece, Rome, Britain, China, Russia, or America, there is no ultimate security or permanence in wealth, power, weapons, monuments, boasting, or even self-chronicling. Freedom is open-ended, so the strong and free are free to squander their strength and freedom, and other individuals and nations are free to rise and challenge them too.

Sustaining individual and political freedom is an art that is demanding and all too rare.

Add these four points together and it becomes clear why the Bible's view of time, history, and human freedom finds itself the odd man out among modern ideas, just as it has done down through the ages. Today it flies in the face of numerous attempts to deny human freedom in one way or another or to sustain it in ways that are counterproductive. Biblically based freedom confounds the smug assumption of scientism that science and scientific knowledge are the sum of all that there is to be known. Freedom defies the imperial overreach of the business manager and the socialist planner who presume that they know all the factors to be taken into account in decision-making for a company or a society. And soon, freedom will make a mockery of the totalitarian tendencies of the futurists who assure us that we can rest secure, trusting in the all-encompassing algorithms of tomorrow, for they will know us better than we know ourselves. Against the handcuff logic of all such views, human freedom will never fail to show that, for better or worse, choice, creativity, and change will always turn out differently than the most confident and certain of predictions.

Open-endedness is sometimes taken as a sly guarantee that things will turn out for better rather than for worse, but that too is wrong. There are no guarantees, and leaders, governments, and others who promise what they cannot guarantee will pay for their hubris in the end. Human open-endedness includes the possibility of stupidity, error, cowardice, ingratitude, backsliding, disobedience, revenge, and hubris as well as bravery, generosity, loyalty, and good faith. In the covenantal perspective on time, nothing is written, but we ourselves are free to write badly, irresponsibly, or not at all. There is no determinism compelling us—

we are responsible, though we ourselves may be determined to do wrong rather than right. If we choose rightly, anything can be reformed and improved, yet there can be no prospect of perfectibility short of the messianic age. We are never surprised when the open-endedness of the human story demonstrates either *the better* or *the worse* with equal clarity.

All this hammers home the need for humility and responsibility rather than hubris. We humans must always be grateful for freedom, and we must respect its mystery. We must be humbled by the power of our freedom and our proneness to corrupt and lose freedom altogether. There is more to knowing than knowing will ever know, and our deepest motives will always be unfathomable, even to ourselves. But at the same time, our choices will always be consequential, so we must stand humbly responsible before God and before the bar of history. The future is partly ours to be made or unmade, and ours is the responsibility for it. Alongside the Jewish people, Christians are called to enter and act in the arena of history, with all the blood, sweat, and tears that such engagement demands. They must have one eye on the world and their times, and another on a hope beyond history.

May I say it again? The glory of time, history, and human freedom in the Jewish and Christian understanding is quite different from almost all other views of human life. We humans are never finally determined by fate, by our stars, by *karma*, by *kismet*, by our genes, by chance or luck, or by any purely scientific determinism or external necessity of nature that becomes "our lot in life." There is no ultimate déjà vu to our existence and no reincarnation or "eternal recurrence" in our lives. To say we are born this way is never a full excuse for what we do. To be sure, we are never completely free, because we are shaped by countless external forces as well as by our own previous choices that have become the habits of our heart and thus our self-chosen character. But because we are never simply *caused*, though strongly influenced, we are still truly and decisively free if only in how we choose to respond to the circumstances in which we find ourselves. History in its flow is singular, and we in the freedom of our lives are significant.

If this view of freedom is a gift and we are consequential and responsible, the downside must clearly be held in mind. Freedom can be used for good or ill, and even corrupted and lost entirely—which means that humans should assert and exercise freedom gratefully, humbly, and responsibly. There is a striking paradox of freedom: freedom can become the greatest enemy of freedom, for the corruption of freedom means that free people can start as masters but end as slaves to their own self-chosen obsessions (addiction to ideas) and to their own self-chosen addictions (obsession with behaviors). Above all, human freedom must never be inflated into hubris. (We are "the Gods of planet earth," says Yuval Noah Harari.)[14]

This need for constant responsibility and humility is exponentially magnified today as we approach the arrival of what C. S. Lewis called "the master generation"—the generation whose choices through genetic and social engineering can shape all future generations *without their knowledge or consent*.[15] Soon, with gene editing and the arrival of advanced artificial intelligence or ultra-intelligence, the consequential character of freedom will be brought into the sharpest possible focus. Soon we will have the power, we are told, to create people according to our will, and to create machines "in our image" that will far transcend the power of our own human intelligence. These machines, the work of our own minds and hands, could then be as free, inscrutable, and unpredictable to us as we are to each other and to the animal world.

In that sense, as long predicted by Irving Good and other experts on artificial intelligence, our humility, our responsibility, and our capacity to corrupt freedom will be exposed as never before. What will be our attitude to such ultra-intelligent machines, and what will theirs be to us? For better or ill, they could indeed be "the final machines" and "the last invention that man need ever make."[16]

THE HIGHEST HUMANISM OF ALL

The Bible's portrayal of humanity is the highest form of "humanism" in the sense of the portrayal and protection of supreme human worth. It stands over against all contemporary expressions of humanism, which either exaggerate or minimize the significance of human beings—of which we have four main varieties today: *secular humanism* ("God is dead" and "man is the measure of all things"), *antihumanism* (movements explicitly rejecting secular humanism as sexist, colonialist, species chauvinist, and so on), *posthumanism* (taking the rejection of secular humanism in the direction of oneness with animals and with nature), and *transhumanism* (taking the rejection of secular humanism in the direction of oneness with technology). In strong contrast to these views, the Bible portrays humanity, even after the fall, as still central to God's high purposes in time and history.

The high humanism of the Bible's view of humanity can be explored from several angles, as a series of trios. First, we humans are uniquely relational and conversational. We live our lives in constant dialogue with *ourselves*, with *others*, and with *God* (even if replacing him with substitutes or seeking to reject him altogether). Second, we humans are uniquely consequential on the earth, because of such qualities as our *awareness*, our *agency*, and our *accountability*. And third, we humans are uniquely central in creation as partners with God in his ongoing purposes in time and

history. We are always small and uncertain junior partners, but our response to God's call opens up the interplay between God's *sovereignty*, our human *significance*, and history's *singularity*.

As creator of time, God is always outside of time and sovereign over time. Under God, there is a distinctive singularity about time and history that parallels the distinctive significance of humans created in the image of God. Human agency and the singularity of history mean that no moment in time will ever be the same as any other moment, which is another reason why the sequence of time is not an ever-repeating cycle. It is a nonrepeating sequence that forms a story with a beginning, a development, and an end. And as with all stories, there will always be surprises and suspense as to how the story twists and turns.

Scientists of all sorts may keep on analyzing the various factors that influence us from the inside and the outside, and pundits and consultants of all sorts will offer fancier and fancier forms of business and political predictions. But forces that influence are not ironclad causes. They need not mean control or compulsion. Nor will they ever lead to complete explanation, so no analysts will ever be able to excuse irresponsibility and no forecasters will ever close the circle and deliver certainty. The freedom (and perversity) of human agency means that we will never fully know what happens until it happens. The outcome is never written. Tomorrow will always be partly unknown. It still remains to be written partly through our choices, and such is the paradox of knowledge that the more we claim to know, the less certain we often become about what will happen next.

This covenantal partnership of human beings with God is awe-inspiring, but it is always under God. "I am I" is the awareness that precedes our human agency, and "under God" and "but God" form the accountability that precedes, overarches, and follows it.

The latter are the backstop behind all our human pretentions, for as always "Man proposes, but God disposes." As Joseph says to his brothers, who did not believe that he had really forgiven them for all the troubles they had caused him, "Therefore, it was not you who sent me here, but God" (Gen 45:8). Or in the words of Shakespeare's Hamlet, "There's a divinity that shapes our ends, rough-hew them how we will."[17]

This linking between divine providence and human partnership, divine initiative and human consent, opens up the view of time as covenantal. Time is covenantal in the sense that those who respond to God's call enter into a binding covenantal agreement with him. God's providence overarches history and reins in human pretentions, but under providence, however small and insignificant we seem, we humans are significant agents for either good or ill. Thus those who respond to God's call, who come to know God and walk with him, become entrepreneurial partners with him in advancing his purposes in the world. We are never more than junior partners, of course, but providence ensures that history has a purpose and a point. The meaning of history is therefore the working out of these covenantal purposes in time, though always far beyond any single generation and far beyond our human understanding.

Seen this way, time and history are not an illusion, and there is no reincarnation or eternal recurrence, as there is for the Hindus, Buddhists, and Nietzsche and his followers. Rather, time and history form the stunningly real arena for human action and change, for the ongoing interactive covenantal partnership with God, and for the drama of the conflict between good and evil. The Genesis account of creation tells us that God looked at the universe he had created and pronounced it "good," and then "very good" (Gen 1:25, 31). But God's verdict on history is different from

God's verdict on creation. Sin has changed everything. Much of history *should have been otherwise*. It was not supposed to be this way. Things have gone wrong, badly wrong, and things are still going wrong. The world needs to be put right, and those who know and love God become his covenanted partners in repairing and restoring the world to the state it was designed to be and one day will be again.

Therein lies the striking consequence of the covenantal view of time and history. Human enterprise has significance and solidity, but as a partnership with God and under God. Apart from God, history—with all its accidents, inequalities, injustices, and its apparent meaninglessness viewed from the inside—might well represent Eliade's "terror." But under and alongside God, history is transformed from terror into task. Those who respond to the call of God are entrepreneurs of life. They follow the way of God and act into time and history, while always aiming beyond time and history. Knowing God, they act by faith in him but with a hope that looks over the horizon of history and time. Such actions are real, decisive, and consequential. Whatever their success or failure appears to be in the short-term, such enterprises and such lives are never in vain.

But once again, life in covenantal time is always "under God" and his providence. Whatever the appearances, there is always a moral limit to human power and its hubris. The effectiveness and success of living by faith is ultimately guaranteed, but the success of the outcome lies beyond the reach of the faithful. The Hebrew prophet's assurance that "The righteous will live by his faith" (Hab 2:4) sounded out not in prosperous and peaceful times but in violent and chaotic times when nothing external seemed to justify such confidence—and certainly nothing that any human could do. In our broken world, many lives may appear insignificant, even forlorn, and many of our lives are "incomplete," for not all the great things that are worth doing can be completed in a single lifetime. (In the words of Rabbi Tarfon, "It is not for you to complete the task, but neither are you free to desist from it.")[18]

But success, achievement, fame, and legacy are not the goal of those who live by faith. The time frame of the *here and now* is too short to be an accurate measure. Men and women of faith act into history, all the time gazing over the edge of the horizon of history, and many times they die with their visions unfulfilled, their successes incomplete, and their legacy unachieved or unclear. But as the writer of the letter to the Hebrews says of such visionaries and entrepreneurs who live by faith and look to God, "God is not ashamed to be called their God; for He has prepared a city for them" (Heb 11:16).

In short, according to the covenantal view of time, and absolutely contrary to Zen Buddhism, each of us is a stone thrown into the pond who causes everlasting ripples in the grand ocean of time and the flow of history.

DIFFERENT CONCEPT, DIFFERENT CALENDAR

Many consequences flow from this covenantal view of time and the primacy of history. They begin with a distinctive sense of the calendar of time and the rhythms of life, but history is unmistakably essential and central to them all. Time for the pagan world and for today's "posthumans" and all the followers of the cyclical view of time is always tied to nature, and to nature looked to as the source of fertility and prosperity. In the ancient world, and in many parts of the world today, reality was understood through myths and rituals, and the year was marked off by festivals that were linked to nature and to the rhythm of its seasons.

Not so with the Bible's view. On the one hand, the Jewish year looked back to creation, and not to nature in any later time period. Time was marked by the Sabbath that celebrated the seventh day of creation, when God climaxed his creation by creating rest as the heart of freedom, peace, and well-being. Few modern people realize that the notion of the seven-day week is the invention of the Bible. There was no such week in the calendar of the ancients. And the theme of the Sabbath's freedom and rest continued through the seven-day and seven-year cycles that climaxed in their completion in the fiftieth year, the year of Jubilee ("Proclaim liberty throughout all the land" [Lev 25:10 KJV]). Long before the time slavery of modern fast life, the link between freedom and rest was strong and central to the covenantal view of time. We humans are truly creative as well as created, but Sabbath is the time-out when we remember the one and forget the other. We cease from our human work, whether creative enterprise or mindless drudgery, in order to remind ourselves that we are neither self-created nor self-sufficient. We are created, and our highest responsibility is to worship our Creator.

On the other hand, the Jewish year looked back to history, rather than nature. The Jewish festivals celebrated the great events though which God had liberated and redeemed his people Israel in history and real time. To be sure, the Jewish festivals took over celebrations that elsewhere were tied to nature, but they transformed them into a celebration of history rather than nature. They commemorated unique, singular, one-off events in real time rather than annually repeated cycles in nature. (The Passover was originally a spring festival, but it was transformed to become a celebration of the exodus from Egypt. Similarly, the Feast of

Weeks was originally a harvest festival but became a celebration of the giving of the Torah, while the Festival of Booths was originally a celebration of the vintage turned into a commemoration of the wilderness sojourning.) In each case, Rabbi Heschel states, "To Israel the unique events of historic time were spiritually more significant than the repetitive processes in the cycle of nature, even though physical sustenance depended on the latter."[19] Thus history and nature come together in the Bible's view, but history provides the ultimate framework of meaning within which creation itself is understood.

The thrust of the Bible's view of time is explosive. In a fallen world, freedom and power will always be abused, and the corruption of freedom will inevitably lead to the corruption of power and then to oppression, injustice, inequality, and domination. Thus the fallen world will always run according to the dark momentum of its remorseless cycles of widening inequality in generation after generation—as the bonded slaves, captive sex workers, dispossessed migrants, and the child warriors all testify in our time. And with the unprecedented fortunes of the superintelligence era, the differentials and divisions between the *haves* and the *have-nots*, the *ens* (the enhanced) and the *uns* (the unenhanced) will only widen and get worse. Among other things, this means that whatever merits are claimed for any political or economic system, whether democracy or free-market capitalism, the outcome will always follow this logic and thus disappoint its enthusiasts and confirm the suspicion and hostility of its critics.

Plainly too, the oppression of today's downward cycle weighs heavily on our sense of time, and no less so for the wealthy than the poor. Modern people become time slaves because so much of our time is under the control of others, and we ourselves squander so much of our lives through the lure of advertising, social media, entertainment, and such diversions as video games and pornography. Modernity makes time slaves of us all.

But whether the world in question is ancient or modern, and whether the problem is power slavery, debt slavery, or time slavery, the Bible counters this negative cycle with a positive and redemptive countercycle—the radical innovation of the Sabbath and the concept of sabbaticals and the Years of Jubilee. Many of us who are Christians, and I include myself, have to admit with shame that we have given little thought to this arrangement and the thinking behind it, and most of us have made nothing of it. Instead, we sway uneasily between almost complete neglect of the notion of Sabbath and sabbaticals and occasional spasms of legalism or guilt at the way we blur all our days in a ceaseless round of work and entertainment.

Yet once again, we and our time-driven world have much to learn from the Bible and our Jewish friends. There is a link, they point out, between Sabbath and the realization of utopia. The notion of u-topia (literally "no place") and the description "utopian" have gained a bad name because they are imaginary. They never arrive, and their advocates are forced to storm the gap between the ideal and the real through violence. The Bible's originality comes in right there to address the interim realistically. "What is unique to Judaism is the sabbatical concept of *utopia now*, a rehearsal every seventh day and seventh year, of an ideal social order in which rest is part of the public domain, available equally to all. . . . It meant that one day in seven all hierarchies of wealth and power were suspended. No one could be forced to work: not employees, or slaves, or even domestic animals." And why? "Those who are servants to God may not be slaves to man"—or to time.[20]

In short, the Sabbath is central to "redeeming the time" in terms of time present, just as repentance and forgiveness are to redeeming the time in terms of time past. As a time-out and a rest, the Sabbath refreshes, restores, and rebalances us. For all our perks and comforts in the modern world, we are more time-driven than ever, but if we follow the threefold arrangement of Sabbath, sabbaticals, and the Jubilee Year, we can reassert rest, refreshment, well-being, and freedom back into time and history every seven days, every seven years, and every fiftieth year, after the long cycle of seven times seven years.

This characteristic break with nature and myth and the insistence on freedom and justice in history are striking and unmistakable features of the Bible. The momentous difference between the covenantal view and the purely cyclical view must never be softened. In the covenantal view, time and history are real, foundational, and inescapable; human agency is real, decisive, and consequential; and the need for an ongoing commitment to freedom and justice is essential. From daily and weekly living to such grand enterprises as science, politics, and the struggle for freedom, justice, and reform, there is no question which view of time and history has shaped the West, and which, for better or worse, has inspired the rise of the modern world and will best lead it forward tomorrow. Rabbi Sacks concludes provocatively but accurately, "Cyclical time is deeply conservative; covenantal time is profoundly revolutionary."[21]

CHRONOLOGICAL TIME

The third major view of time, which is that of the secularist family of faiths, is chronological time. In essence, chronological time is linear and covenantal time shorn of its belief in God, transcendence, eternity, and the supernatural, and thus secularized. If the advocates of cyclical time view *eternity within time*, as in the bliss of Eastern meditation, the advocates of chronological time do the opposite. They view *time without eternity* at all. The Greek word *chronos* was used to personify time. It meant time viewed as a succession of linear moments in contrast to time as *kairos*, which meant time as the significance of a moment that is ripe with meaning and a potential for good or ill.

As a mere succession of linear moments with no inherent meaning, *chronos* is the endless, unvarying, and monotonous ticktock of clock time. It is quite different from *kairos* as the significance of the moment—as, for example, in moments of triumph or disaster that ever after are viewed as "timeless." For some years I attended a church in London where Roger Bannister was a member. On May 6, 1954, in Oxford, he had been the first man in history to run the mile in under four minutes, and for all his later successes in medical science he was forever defined by those four minutes. For most of us, a four-minute segment of life would mean little, but Bannister made no secret of the fact that he wished he had made his name as a researcher. However, he could never transcend those four minutes. He even used to joke about it. "I don't think many people have had the life I enjoyed for four minutes work!" At the time he had described the last few agonizing seconds as "never-ending," but sixty years later he said it "seemed an eternity."

Covenantal time in the Bible is rich with *kairos* moments, for *under God* the drama of history takes on its highest and deepest meaning. Like an old black-and-white film given color or a darkening room with the light switched on, everything looks different in the light of eternity. Famously, for example, Queen Esther's cousin Mordecai challenged her in words that have become legendary, "Who knows whether you have not attained royalty for such a time as this?" (Esther 4:14). But *kairos* time is not unique to the Bible. Shakespeare captured it in the famous words of Mark Anthony's funeral oration in Shakespeare's *Julius Caesar*. "There is a tide in the affairs of men, which taken at the flood leads on to fortune. Omitted, all the voyage of their lives is bound in shallows and in miseries."[22]

The crucial difference between covenantal time and purely chronological time stems from the difference between their two sources of meaning. Meaning from the perspective of covenantal time is finally meaning as God sees and knows it to be (*sub specie aeternitatis*, "under the perspective of eternity"), whereas meaning within chronological time is meaning as humans see it and seek to establish it. This difference is in fact all-important because it divides proponents of chronological linear time into two parties: the optimists who regard self-created human meaning as an entirely feasible project, and the pessimists who don't.

The optimistic party was the child of the eighteenth-century Enlightenment. "God was dead," as Nietzsche expressed it a century later, but there was no need for God any longer. Humanity could take over everything for which God once stood, and humans could sustain and steer their future by themselves. No longer relying on God, nature, or evolution, humanity could now control its own evolution. Human dignity, truth, freedom, reason, science, progress—all these may have been the gifts of the Jewish and Christian Scriptures, but reason could replace revelation and the rest would fall into place in a new and improved secularist march of time and history. Humanity would take over from God, evolution would replace creation, progress in time and history would stand in for heaven and build a new heaven on earth, and moral progress would march hand in hand with technological progress. There would be just as much meaning, purpose, and dynamism as before, a steady human march toward broad and sunlit uplands, but now the meaning would be humanist and self-created and the progress self-sustaining.

In Bertrand Russell's words, a "scientific philosophy" could fashion a "new morality" that would "turn our earth into a paradise."[23] "Modern technics," he declared, "is giving man a sense of power which is changing his whole mentality. . . . It may be that God made the world, but there is no reason why we should not make it over."[24] Or as Lewis Mumford expressed it in *Technics and Civilization*, "Impossible? No; for however far modern science and technics have fallen short, they have taught mankind at least one lesson: Nothing is impossible."[25] The Promethean drive of such attitudes, or the extravagant dream of human omnipotence, is unmistakable in Joseph Proudhon: "We attain to science and society in spite of God. Every progress is a victory in which we crush the Deity."[26]

Humanity would steer linear time toward its own human ends and be the captain of its own fate. Whatever history may have been in the past was past. History by humanity and for humanity would be the arena for human redemption in the present and the future. History would be the story of humanity's unbroken pursuit of freedom, power, and expansion. Faith in God could be jettisoned safely. Indeed, faith in God had to be jettisoned because such notions as providence were the relics and reminders of an earlier time when human minds were still ignorant and human wills impotent.

Russell did not go on to say how this happy vision would be achieved, and there was a simple problem with all the optimistic versions of humanly redeeming history. They didn't happen, they still haven't happened, and when secularism gained power quite the reverse happened. And there were those who saw, early on, that they would not happen. In the early nineteenth century the great Spanish artist Goya detailed his dark warning in his art: "The dream of reason produces monsters." He has been seconded in our own time by John Ralston Saul and his magisterial *Voltaire's Bastards*. Two centuries after Goya, there is no doubt about the uncomfortable link between the Enlightenment and such monsters as racism and eugenics, Auschwitz and the Killing Fields of Cambodia. (For example, Immanuel Kant, the greatest of the Enlightenment philosophers, described the Jews as the "vampires of society" and called for the "euthanasia of Judaism." And Arthur Schopenhauer spoke similarly of Jews as "no better than cattle.")[27]

There are still notable optimists in the secularist camp, such as Harvard's Steven Pinker with the soaring hopes of his titles such as *Enlightenment Now* and *The Better Angels of Our Nature*. But the ranks of the optimists and those who believe in redeeming history are far thinner today, and the weight of evidence now favors the greater realism of other atheists. Technological progress has been breathtaking, but it appears that moral progress has been winded and left panting by the roadside. Worse still, as critics such as Reinhold Niebuhr charged, uncritical confidence in a limitless expansion of human freedom and in history as the arena for human redemption heightened the headlong dynamism of Western civilization to the point where "it became a kind of demonic fury."[28]

Perhaps the last best hope for a renewal of eighteenth-century-style optimism lies with transhumanism and the hopes for ultra-intelligence. There is certainly no question that the transhumanist visions for the techno-liberation of humanity in the future are soaring. For example, in his *Life 3.0*, Max Tegmark claims that superintelligence will not only transform humanity but wake up the entire universe to give it meaning and consciousness. It will transform

> our Universe from a mindless zombie with no self-awareness into a living ecosystem harboring self-reflection, beauty and hope—and the pursuit of goals, meaning and purpose. Had

our Universe never awoken, then, as far as I am concerned, it would have been completely pointless—merely a gigantic waste of space. Should our Universe go back to sleep due to some cosmic calamity or self-inflicted mishap, it will, alas, become meaningless.[29]

Yet which is more stunning, we might ask, Tegmark's summary dismissal of any meaning in the universe over the last many billions of years or his stunningly sunny optimism that the next generation will light up all life and the entire universe with meaning it has never had until these brave new technosaviors were born to spread their beneficence throughout the cosmos?

For the moment, however, philosopher John Gray, a leading atheist himself, has delivered a triple blow to all the present varieties of Enlightenment optimism—liberal democratic, secular progressive, neo-Marxist, or whatever. First, he notes that the liberal atheism that believes in humanist progress is a "late flower of the Jewish and Christian religion, and in the past most atheists have not been liberals."[30] (Atheism in its modern form, we might say, could not flourish without the church—it is either a parasite on the best of Christian truths or a protest against the worst of Christian behavior). Second, Gray argues that many of the Enlightenment thinkers were themselves guilty of egregious evils, such as the blatant racism of Voltaire, David Hume, H. G. Wells, and Julian Huxley, and the horrifying eugenics of Margaret Sanger. And third, he demonstrates the embarrassing link between secularism and the violence and oppression of the last century, and between the Enlightenment and modern anti-Semitism.

Gray's conclusion is unsparing, if provocative: "If you want to understand atheism and religion, you must forget the popular notion that they are opposites. . . . Contemporary atheism is a continuation of monotheism by other means. Hence the unending succession of God-surrogates, such as humanity and science, technology and the all-too-human visions of transhumanism."[31]

THE PARTY OF PESSIMISM

The pessimistic party has long argued for a darker estimate of chronological linear time. If life is short, we only go around once, and time is merely a succession of moments with no discernible beginning, no known successful ending, and no given meaning, what does it add up to? What sort of story has no beginning and no end? How are we supposed to look on the journey or voyage of life if we don't know how it started, and we don't know where it is going? What would film-going be like if we were always condemned to see no more than a few minutes in the middle of a film? The best we could do would be no better than guesswork. That is the dilemma that Milan Kundera pitted against the Eastern and Nietzschean view. Karma and "eternal recurrence" mean that there is an oppressive weightiness to every action because we are condemned to repeat the actions forever, but the opposite view leads to "an unbearable lightness of being." As Kundera's protagonist Tomas asks in his novel by the same title, "What can life be worth if the first rehearsal is life itself?" After all, "If we only have one life to live, we might as well have not lived at all."[32]

Do we really have to pretend that while there is no ultimate meaning in the universe, the search itself is somehow an adequate meaning and not futile? What difference is there between such pointlessness and hopelessness? Paul Gauguin, the French postimpressionist artist, raised such questions in his famous painting from Tahiti: *Where Do We Come From? What Are We? Where Are We Going?* Read from right to left, he portrayed his vision of the passages of life, ending with an old woman near death and a strange bird, representing the uselessness of words.

Later in the last century, the Irish playwright Samuel Beckett became the poet of the meaninglessness of chronological linear time. In his play *Waiting for Godot*, one of the two tramps made an early remark that aptly summarizes the pointlessness that pervades the play like a fog: "Nothing to be done." The spawn of such pointlessness is not so much suicide as terminal lethargy.

In a later play, *Krapp's Last Tape*, Beckett deepens the devastation of chronological time without meaning even more fiercely. A sixty-nine-year-old man listens to tapes of himself that he recorded as a young man in his twenties and thirties. They are unrecognizable to him. He has become a different man. But then who was he, and who is he? Without any overarching meaning or continuity, the relentless flow of the succession of the moments has shattered his life and his identity into fragments. The meaningless succession of moments had smashed his identity into a thousand disconnected points in time. Heraclitus's famous saying that "you cannot step into the same river twice" is usually only half understood. Not only will the river be a different river when you step in it again, but you yourself will not be the same person who stepped into it before.

If there is no meaning to time and history, considered purely chronologically, then Shakespeare's Macbeth was right all along. Life is only "a tale told by an idiot." Or as Joseph Heller's Bruce Gold expressed it, "History is a trash bag of random coincidences blown open by the wind."[33] This view surely takes us back to Eliade's random and meaningless "history as terror"—though most people simply duck the conclusion by not thinking about it. Our ancestors who believed in cyclical time may have been pessimistic in their conclusion, but at least they were realistic. Modern people, by contrast, tend to be escapist, surrounding themselves with diversions and euphemisms.

But make no mistake. Modern secular people have to be escapist because only the few really face the logic of the alternative. Art historian John Berger comments from the vantage point of the secular and merely chronological, and strikingly leaves out the biblical view: we face "the finality of modern despair." In earlier worldviews, "time was cyclic and this meant that the 'ideal' original state would one day return or was retrievable. . . . With entropy and the nineteenth century view of time, we face only the irretrievable and dissipation."[34]

Sooner or later the choice between these views of time will suddenly loom large for each of us and become a matter of life and death. For any who follow the wisdom of the ages regarding humanity and time, they will come to a crossroads. "Under the sun," as the ancient Hebrew text puts it, there is only "Meaningless, meaningless, everything is meaningless" (Eccles 1:2 NIV). Brief, brief breath. Brief, brief breath. All is but a brief, brief breath and then nothing.

Do we at that point stick to the secular and chronological road to nowhere, do we turn off to the Eastern path and renounce this ever-circling world as an illusion from which we must escape, or do we turn back to the biblical view of covenantal time through which both history and our human freedom gain a peerless significance? Contrast is the mother of clarity. Entire worlds and ways of life grow out of each view. From our own individual hopes for personal freedom to the great questions surrounding the future of free societies, it is clear that the stakes are immense. Time, history, meaning, significance, and the character of civilization are all at stake in the view we choose and the view of the world that we live within.

SURVIVAL OF THE FASTEST

THE CLOCK, IT IS SAID, IS THE MOST powerful and consequential invention of the Western world. Through the clock, technology now appears to be taking over from faith and philosophy as the primary shaper of time in human experience. The clock is essential to understanding the modern world itself, but certainly to understanding time in the modern world. And the present moment is an excellent time to attempt to assess it. One of the advantages of our global era is that we now have a heightened awareness of all the world's cultures, including their different attitudes to time. Among other things, this allows each part of the world to compare itself with other cultures and so to see itself as it might not have done earlier. Previously each culture was more isolated and its ways of life were almost the only way life and all it knew.

Take the West and its knowledge of Islam, for example. The first months after the September 11 terrorist attacks on New York were like a crash course in the history of the relationship between the West and Islam. Various dates were flashed across the screen of public consciousness: AD 732 and the battle of Tours when the Islamic tide almost reached to the gates of Paris; 1492 and the defeat of the Moors in Spain; September 11, 1683, when the last Muslim forces were repulsed at the siege of Vienna; and 1798 when General Napoleon Bonaparte landed in Egypt and subjected the heartlands of the Muslim world to Western military dominance.

But in fact the real conquest of the Near East began far earlier, and the invader was neither a crusader nor a general, a diplomat, or a missionary. Interestingly, it was a Western machine, which has been called "the mother of machines" and even "the ultimate missionary machine"—the clock. The mechanical clock was invented in Europe around AD 1400. It was pivotal to the rise of the modern world and therefore to our consciousness of time in the modern world and to the impact of the modern world on the rest of the world. "The clock did not man make," an African saying runs. But the clock was certainly instrumental in the making of modern man and woman. Not only is it infinitely more influential than well-known carriers of globalization such as Coca-Cola, McDonald's, and MTV. It is also the catalyst—or culprit—behind the pressures of modern time on us and our views of the present and the future.

By and large the Muslim world was resistant and slow to adapt to mechanical clocks, just as the Chinese welcomed them at once but kept them as toys for the emperor rather than as tools for the whole of society. In the seventeenth century the English diarist John Evelyn quotes a traveler as saying that the Persians "had neither clocks nor watches." As late as 1947, a French visitor to the Near East remarked that he made a point of being late for appointments on the advice of his hosts, who said, "Here the sky is too blue, the sun too hot. Why hurry? Why do injury to the sweetness of living?"

Today, when globalization is bringing the modern Western view of time to the whole world, the contrast between traditional and modern views is captured in a hundred homespun sayings from people outside the West. Filipinos, for instance: "Westerners are people with gods on their wrists," though with smartphones it would be "in our palms." Or Kenyans: "All Westerners have watches. Africans have time." It is precisely this modern view of time—clock time—that we must understand if we are to escape its worst effects while simultaneously reasserting the importance of humanness.

Choice and change are at the very heart of the modern world. From manufacturers to marketers, from smorgasbords to supermarkets and shopping catalogs, choice is paraded before us in an endless variety of ways. So when it comes to clocks and watches, we are so used to our options that we don't notice the things over which we have no choice. Do you want a Rolex, an Omega, or a Swatch? A watch that is analog or digital? A traditional or a contemporary style? A watch that's self-winding, battery-driven, or solar powered? Do you want it to be gold or stainless steel? Do you want your alarm to ring or play music? Do you want to wake up at once or to be able to press the snooze button? Do you need your watch to tell you your blood pressure and how many steps you have taken today?

In areas like these, the choices go on and on, and the ads and commercials of the world testify to the ubiquitous passion for watches of all kinds, the astronomical prices some people are willing to pay—constrained only by money and fashion. Choice, after all, is the birthright of the modern consumer. But such options are actually the trivial faces of modern time. Far more important are the features we can neither choose nor change. In particular, for better or for worse, three features of modern clock time decisively shape our lives and our thinking. Here, as so often, if we are to withstand, we must understand.

PRECISION

The first feature of modern clock time is precision. Time and space are the two basic elements in which we live and move as human beings. So the measurement of time is essential to human life as we master nature and take control of our world. Of course, there were ways to measure time before the invention of the clock. But these old ways of measurement were largely seasonal and spiritual, and they were always imprecise.

Three important developments lay behind the modern sense of clock time: First, there was a shift from the lunar calendar, which depends only on observation, to the solar calendar, which depends on calculation. Second, there was a shift from a natural sense of time, as in days, to an artificial sense of time, as in weeks. Third, there was a shift from a sense of broad periods, as in morning and afternoon, to a sense of greater precision, as in hours, minutes, and seconds.

The invention of the mechanical clock was decisive in the rise of the modern world. All the various instruments in use before it were slow and restricted. Without the sun, for instance, the sundial was useless—which made it useless at night and limited in countries with short days or bad weather. The Greeks and the Italians obviously had a great advantage over the Norwegians and the Scots. Equally, the slightest leak or any irregular flow in a water clock made it unreliable or put it out of action. And obviously too, the hourglass had to be turned over precisely as the last grain of sand ran from the top to the bottom if it was to mark more than one hour with any accuracy.

All that was changed by the clock. Not only was the mechanical clock the first important all-metal machine, it was also an instrument for all seasons, all weathers, and all hours of the day and night. Above all, the clock gained power when the technology of the early devices called escapements was replaced by pendulums, and then by seconds pendulums in the seventeenth century (which gave rise to the familiar "ticktock" sound), and then by main springs, and finally by the rise of the quartz clock and the atomic clock. Today, scientists can measure time to the accuracy of 9,192,631,770 quantum vibrations of an atom of cesium per second. (My local watch shop greets me with the offer of a watch that is accurate to within a second every million years, but the latest atomic clocks can make that a second every billion years.) Clearly, the clock is a force for precision that is unrivaled in human history.

Whether measuring in light years or nanoseconds, we can now measure anywhere and everywhere in the entire universe. The result is a split-second precision in timing that the traditional world would have found astonishing. Precise time is a universal means of measurement and one of the greatest innovations in the history of humankind. When the American explorers Lewis and Clark traveled west, they arranged to meet at a certain place on a certain date, and eventually met nine days later—which they described as "relatively punctual." Such imprecision would be disastrous for, say, docking at a space station, but quite unnecessary too.

Naturally, as modern people we take this precision for granted, just as we take the air we breathe for granted. Ours is a world in which lawyers and psychiatrists charge by the hour, telephone companies bill by the minute and second, television networks charge advertisers by the second, Olympic athletes win or lose by hundredths of a second, and astronauts execute their life-and-death maneuvers in nanoseconds. There are certainly cultural variations in how punctual we wish to be—between, say, the precision of Switzerland and the studied delay of some Latin countries where to be punctual would be gauche. But whenever we need and want to be, we can be precise, precise, precise. And in this world of modern precision, punctuality has become a virtue in its own right, and unpunctuality a vice or a tacit statement of ego or status.

COORDINATION

The second feature of modern clock time is a central consequence of precision—coordination. Coordination of time sounds obvious and easy, and as one might expect, Coordinated Universal Time is centrally directed in grand bureaucratic fashion today—by the International Bureau of Weights and Measures in Sèvres near Paris. In the global era, a second must be the same second in Paris, New York, Beijing, Johannesburg, and Rio de Janeiro, just as for meters and kilos. But such coordination and such "correct time" are actually a very recent idea. Seneca captured the original diversity of times in his remark, "One can expect an agreement between philosophers sooner than between clocks."[1]

As a moment's thought makes obvious, a precise sense of time is essential not only to science and technology. It is also influential for ordinary life, above all in planning and coordinating our daily affairs. Much of the best and most basic in our daily lives pivots on timing and fitting in with others—getting up in the morning, meeting friends, keeping appointments, catching planes, fulfilling deadlines, expecting deliveries, watching the news, or arriving for a wedding on time. No devotee of any ancient religion could rival us as modern people in our instant, total obedience to the "gods on our wrists" (or in our palms) that send us scurrying from one appointment to the next—always hurrying around and never caught up.

It is said that a central feature of the Western world is "polyphony"—the harmony we achieve through balancing unity and diversity and through blending different parts to give them a common purpose. Such polyphony can be heard in our Western music (for example, in choirs), in our politics (for example, in different parties under law), and in our sports (for example, with keen rivals competing within the same rules). But the key component of this coordination is clock time, for the precision of clock time is what makes possible the plans, schedules, timetables, and logistics of the modern world.

Before the rise of the modern world, different villages, towns, and cities lived happily with their own sense of time, even if they were within what we know as the same time zone today. This began to change in the early industrial era. Coordination in time began to spread, and its supreme symbols were the railway and its timetable. Suddenly the nineteenth-century world exploded and contracted at the same time. Whole continents were crisscrossed with lines of communication called railway tracks, and little puffing engines industriously ran to and fro according to giant station clocks and weighty railway timetables. Swiss trains, for example, have always run with the smoothness, efficiency, and cleanliness of Swiss watches. You can set your watch by a Swiss train. Their coordination is so smooth and efficient that they represent the highest standards of precise coordination.

In our day, airports have often replaced train stations, computers have taken over from stationmasters and timetables,

atomic accuracy has done away with ponderous Victorian time-
pieces, and we are awash with jargon such as "access," "connec-
tivity," and "networking." But when things go well, we still say
that "they run like clockwork."

PRESSURE

The third feature of modern clock time is the one we are most
aware of and which is reinforced by coordination—pressure.
Today at the high noon of modern life, time in the clock-driven
world has become so precise and coordinated that it's all around
us, driving us from behind, pulling us from in front, pressing us
from above, and squeezing us from all sides. The gods on our wrists
have become, in the words of Charles Baudelaire, "the sinister god."
As the nineteenth-century French poet protested in his poem "The
Clock," "3,600 times per hour, the second whispers: Remember!"

If we want to, we can still speak of "killing time" or "doing
time"—the first phrase meaning a voluntary and the second an
involuntary passing of time when time's passage is its only object.
But for most of us, such attitudes to time are rare. After childhood,
in fact, there are very few periods when the clock goes too slow for
us and far too many when it goes too fast. To be sure, a few sharp
observers saw the effects of measured time and protested early on.
The Roman playwright Plautus, for example, wrote in 200 BC, "The
gods confound the man who first found out how to distinguish
hours! Confound him, too, who in this place first set up a sun dial,
to cut and hack my days so wretchedly into small portions."

Two millennia later, we can all sympathize with the poet's com-
plaint. Time-drivenness is our daily reality. "Harried and hurried"
is our daily way of life now. "Fretting and fussing" has become
our chronic condition. Six centuries after the invention of the

clock, the idea of time-keeping has become a euphemism and the idea of time-saving a joke. The ticktock, ticktock of Father Time has become the background drumbeat and staccato bark of the drill sergeant who drives us across the parade ground of life.

No wonder our fast life is a marginless world of 24/7/365 living. In 1751, novelist Henry Fielding was the first to write that "time is money." Today, time is big money and scarce money. So we *buy time*, *maximize time*, and make sure we are having *quality time*. We figure out the opportunity costs of all we do. We become adept at multitasking. We press life to the edges and make the most of every spare second we have—with *split-screen news* packing in the information for us, *on-hold advertising* filling in the empty seconds, and *professional queue-ers* who stand in line for others to save them the unwanted tax on their time that bureaucrats love to impose. In such a world, efficiency is a supreme virtue and seconds are "the currency of modern life."[2]

For those in the fast lane of the fast life of the modern world, life is fired at us point-blank. Everything seems to be happening all at once, so much so that we not only expect it, we require it as an adrenaline rush. Change has to be unceasing, voices have to be rudely grabbing, the music in shops and restaurants has to be blaring, and the latest has to be replaced instantly by the newest and latest. All this has gone so far and become so natural that for many people, jam-packed eventfulness is a necessity and attention deficit disorder a common condition.

If it were possible, time and motion experts would like to rationalize every last second of our days so that we could be even more efficient and productive—even in our leisure. At the beginning of the age of mass production, Henry Ford said of his ideal worker, "He must have every second necessary, but not a single unnecessary second." Was he being generous or ruthless? It all depends on the standard by which you judge what you believe is necessary—but the standard is efficiency.

All this means that the underlying modern attitude to time is plain: pressure, pressure, pressure. Too much fast food may lead to the slow-food movement, and wall-to-wall busyness may drive a sharp rise in time-out practices such as meditation, yoga, and mindfulness. But the latter are only reactions and diversions, not solutions. All they do is provide moments in which we can catch our breath before plunging back into the surging whitewater of fast life that is unrelenting and unstoppable.

Time is life's ultimate credit card today, speed is the universal style of spending, and the-faster-the-better is the ideal tempo of life. Call it craziness, call it the curse of our age, or call it the tyranny of the urgent. Call it anything you like, but it is impossible to stop the world today, even if you want to get off. This manic speed is affecting our blood pressure, shaping our daily experience, and challenging our understanding of what carpe diem means and how we are to "seize the day" and make the most of our short lives.

THE HIDDEN
TYRANNY
OF TIME

GEORGE ORWELL ONCE REMARKED, "We have now sunk to the depth where the restatement of the obvious is the first duty of intelligent men." In that sense, the last chapter was merely putting into words what we all know instinctively. Features of modern time such as precision, coordination, and pressure are obvious once we pause to think about them—though we rarely do because we rarely have the time. Time in the modern world is like that: not only all around us but coming at us from all sides and hard to figure out as it pummels us and regulates our days.

Describing the fast life of modern time has a certain value, but we have to go further. Modern time has deeper features that we must delve into as well. They are not as obvious as the features we looked at, but they are equally vital. In fact, they are the real tyrannies of time in our world, and they are especially important for people who wish to think independently and live with integrity.

THE POWER OF LABELING

The first deeper power of our modern view of time is its power to label and thus to define and shape reality. Words are handles or labels that we stick on reality. They are greatly influential because the way we say things shapes the way we see things. Say something often enough and eventually we'll come to see it that way. Before long, even something startling and unusual will become routine and self-evident. Our use of nicknames and name-calling are obvious examples. The words exert power. Call someone a "beanpole" or a "dummy" and people aren't likely to expect them to be overweight or blessed with a surfeit of gray cells. Say something often enough and eventually we will all come to see it that way.

The words we use to speak about time are the same, and they are all the more powerful because they go unnoticed. Embedded in our daily language, they shape and furnish our view of time, and thus direct and mold our experience of time itself. For instance, one of the strongest effects of the clock was that the universe began to be seen as one gigantic clock. In the words of the seventeenth-century scientist Robert Boyle, at the birth of early modern science the universe was "a great piece of clock work." Modern views have replaced this early modern view, but the powerful, subliminal impact of clocks and clock time still moves through our language to shape our view of reality. It may be heard at two points in particular.

FROM SPACE TO TIME

One point is the way in which words that once referred to space now refer to time. The word *civilized*, for example, used to have a spatial element at its core. A key to the distinction between civilized and uncivilized used to be the idea of being *beyond* in terms of space. If some group saw itself as civilized, then those beyond the circle of their society were uncivilized. They were "beyond the pale." Most famously the Greeks saw themselves as civilized, while all who were outside the circle of their enlightenment were barbarians.

This measuring stick has been transformed by the rise of clocks and clock time. The uncivilized are no longer beyond in terms of space but behind in terms of time. They are no longer barbarians but primitives, reactionaries, and Neanderthals. The means of measurement is now one of years and periods rather than miles and boundaries. As advertisers at the turn of the new millennium said archly in a show of chronological snobbery, highlighting the new by scorning the old and passé, "That was so twentieth century." At a more serious level, John Stuart Mill, the great champion of liberalism, restricted freedom to "human beings in the maturity of their facultie," and therefore excluded children and "the backward states of society."[1] And at an even deadlier level, the Bolsheviks used time as a standard to discount people altogether. In "The Declaration of the Rights of Toiling and Exploited People," which was a founding text of the Soviet Union in January 1918, Lenin purged remnants of the old regime by disenfranchising them as "former people."[2]

Another example of words that now refer to time rather than space is the term *progress*. In its early use it referred to space, but now it almost always refers to time. Thus John Bunyan's "pilgrim's progress" meant a journey, and a king's progress once meant a royal procession or parade along a road—more like the movement of a carnival float or a Macy's Thanksgiving Day Parade than a scientific discovery or a growth in proficiency or maturity. The latter, of course, would be more common today. *Progress*, *progressive*, and their opposites, *reactionary*, *passé*, and *old-fashioned* are more likely to refer to advances or set-backs in science, technology, and civil rights—and always movement in terms of time rather than space. This has become fateful in both the realm of politics and the realm of faith because progress is taken as automatically and self-evidently positive—*regardless of the content of what is being proposed under its banner*. For modern people, the sheer claim to progress is argument enough.

PRESCRIPTION, NOT DESCRIPTION

The powerful, subliminal impact of clocks and clock time can be heard at a second point—the way in which words smuggle in evaluation in the guise of description. They pretend to describe, but in fact they praise or disparage. This is already clear in the examples above. *Progress* purports to describe an advance but it also pronounces it good. The evaluation is mixed in with the description and it's impossible to take it back.

For those who subscribe to progressivism—and in a sense technology makes us all progressives now—progress by definition is good, always good, self-evidently good, unquestionably good. Reaction, by definition, is bad. According to the improvement myth of the Enlightenment creed, the world is getting better and better. Whatever *is* today is not only right but a great deal better than what was yesterday. And of course, whatever is coming must be a great deal better still. The word *progress* simply makes it so and tells us so. We are not asked to think. We are not even given the opportunity or the criteria to judge for ourselves. If it's progressive, by definition it must be good. If it's reactionary, it obviously must be bad, and that's the end of it. Discussion over.

The same power of smuggled judgments can be heard in words describing periods of history. For example, the standard labels Dark Ages, Middle Ages, and Modern Age were first used in the early days of the modern era. To any of us who doesn't know these ages as the historian does, the suggestion is clear. There was little of worth in the earlier period, and the value of the second period is that it leads to the climax of all the developments, the modern era.

In other words, "all roads lead to Rome" and all periods of history point to us, right now, for are we not the climax of history? Just keep saying the words and their power will flatter us into believing them. After all, if "the newer is the truer" and "the latest is the greatest," we in this generation are the consummation of the ages. We are the apex of history, and we can forget the qualifying words *so far*. Clearly, the purpose of history is us, and the present moment is the occasion to break out the champagne and make a toast to ourselves.

PRESUMPTION

The second hidden consequence of modern time is presumption. Our modern words about time have a built-in preference and bias, but the preference is left unstated and the bias unargued. Like an emperor whose writ is absolute within his empire, the unexamined tyranny of modern time imposes its perspectives and preferences on all who live within its sway. Surely and beyond all question, it presumes, this way of seeing things is quite simply the way things are.

The words *progress*, *progressives*, and *progressivism* are clear examples of presumption as well as of labeling. Needless to say such terms are perfectly legitimate if there is a clear idea of th standards by which progress can be judged—for they assume and require certain conceptions of the good, the true, the just, the beautiful, and the mature. By such standards, which will vary for different people, we are able to judge what they consider to be progress and what is slippage or decline. But if there is no standard, the notion of *progressive* quickly becomes a cosmological myth. In fact, it becomes a cosmological myth on a par with the myths of the ancient world.

A clear standard is rarely the case with the current political use of the terms, when *progressive* is the magical password that opens the door to any and every political position regardless of whether it is true or false, wise or foolish, practical or utopian. Thus *progressive* is the alias and the alibi for postmodernism, political correctness, socialism, social constructionism, cultural Marxism, the sexual revolution, and the like. If they are progressive, who needs to think about them? The term itself stands or falls by the prestige of the Enlightenment belief in continuous advance, which is taken as solid, self-evident, and proven. For some of its proponents, progress is achieved through the state (for those on the left), while for others it is through the market (for those in the center or on the right), or through science and technology (for everyone, but the elites above all).

For the ancient world, what sociologist Peter Berger called its "sacred canopy" was provided by the various cosmological myths, such as the Babylonian belief in Marduk and the Greek belief in Zeus, Apollo, and Athene. Today, however, progressivism has become the sacred canopy of the secular left. For the ancients the various cosmological myths loaned strength to individuals as "the representative of the gods." For the secular modern left, the progressive myth tells people that whatever they claim to be doing is justified because they are on "the right side of history."

Yet as stressed earlier, the Enlightenment's belief in continuous improvement and advance is no longer credible. It has stalled, and it did nothing to prevent the horrors of the Holocaust, the world wars, and the genocides in the twentieth century. Whether the progress hoped for was for human advance in general or the dream of economic betterment in particular, the evident frustration and cynicism in the younger generation stem from their bitter conclusion: The promised future may not be better than the past, yet the term *progressive* is still flaunted as self-evident.

Beyond this foundational weakness, there are theoretical flaws in the terms now used—and, once again, regardless of the content. First, the claim for "progress" was a parasite on the biblical view of time and hope, which is why progressives provided no standard by which to judge the progress they claimed. Aside from the positive connotations of the bare word *progress*, the term *progressive* could as easily be *regressive*, for some of its "achievements," such as the expanded state, are a step backwards for personal freedom, not forward. G. K. Chesterton noted this inherent problem when he remarked, "progress is simply a comparative of which we have not settled the superlative."[3] T. S. Eliot remarked similarly on "an age which advances progressively backwards."[4] John Gray even describes secular humanism as a "sacred relic," in the sense that the humanist view of progress was based squarely on the Jewish and Christian view. "The belief that humans are gradually improving is the central article of faith of modern humanism. When wrenched from monotheistic religion, however, it is not so much false as meaningless."[5]

Second, the term *progressive* quickly becomes a form of self-congratulation. As Gray charges, "When secular thinkers tell th story of humankind as a story of progress they flatter the selves that they embody the progress of which they spea

From Auguste Comte's "organic society" to Marx's "communism" to Herbert Spencer's "minimal government" to Francis Fuku-yama's liberal democracy as "the end of history," each of them toasted themselves as the climax of the ages and therefore an-nounced that history had reached its culmination in the form of society that they favored—only for history to move on and leave them stranded and with egg on their faces.

Third, most progressives lack the philosophical assumptions that progressivism needs to justify itself. Often their assumptions betray them. President Obama and many American progressives often quote Martin Luther King Jr., who was quoting Theodore Parker from the nineteenth century: "The arc of the moral uni-verse is long, but it bends towards justice." But in the very speech when King used this phrase, in his sermon from the Torah at Temple Israel of Hollywood in February 1965, he pointed out that many people do not have the assumptions to undergird such a confident view of progress. Their idea of progress is no better than the notion King attacked, citing Thoreau, as "improved means to an unimproved end."[7] When left-wing progressives breezily claim to be on the "right side of history" and consign their opponents to "the dustbin of history," they simply cannot justify their claims from either the past or the present. Indeed, they have no more credibility than Nikita Khrushchev when he angrily pounded the podium at the United Nations with his shoe and shouted, "Whether you like it or not, history is on our side. We will bury you!"

Fourth, progressivism often takes over from monotheism an absolutist and militant view of truth, but usually without the values or correctives of the latter at its best. Once again, Gray is sparing in his warning: "Any way of life that fails or refuses to into a story of progress can be regarded as subhuman, exiled to the margins of history and then consigned to extinction."[8] Nazism and communism provide unmistakable examples, but the rhetoric of many left-wing movements in the West displays the same logic of intolerant tolerance. Indeed, Gray concludes, "If monotheism gave birth to liberal values, a militant secular version of the faith may usher in their end."[9]

Such is the power of hope, of course, that in good times the appeal of the progressive attitude will always be stronger than its rationale. And what affects politics is the progressive attitude and in particular the overspill from its disdain for the past. Secretary of State Dean Acheson's remark to a prominent European summed up the prejudice perfectly, but also revealed how progressivism will be the poisoned chalice for the American republic in the future: "Looking back," he said, "the gravest problem I had to deal with was how to steer, in this atomic age, the foreign policy of a world power saddled with the constitution of a small, eighteenth-century farmers' republic."[10]

A generation after Acheson, the progressive problem has become worse in America because the standard to judge the "progress" has changed decisively, though many have yet to realize it. Following the "seismic Sixties," many left-wing progressives promote ideas that owe more to 1789, the French Revolution and its heirs, than they do to 1776 and the ideas and ideals of the American Revolution. As such, too many public intellectuals in America are on a collision course with the roots of their own great experiment in freedom. Yet while some are well aware of the different views they are pursuing, others are blind to how they have become the latest variation in the *trahison des clercs* ("the betrayal of the intellectuals").

Why "betrayal"? Surely that is too strong a word. We should remember that history's first official social critics were the He prophets, who had a key role in Israel's, and therefore history's, earliest "separation of powers." Standing over against the power of the kings and the power of the priests, the prophets had a dual task. First, and more positively, their responsibility was to keep calling the nation back to the ideals and terms of Israel's founding constitution, the covenant. Second, and more negatively, their equal responsibility was to challenge any and all forms of the corruptions of power, whether by the kings, the priests, the people, or the false prophets.

This dual calling of the prophets was critical to the ongoing character and existence of the Jewish people, and there is surely a parallel responsibility for public intellectuals today. Their responsibility is to call their nations to live up to their ideals and to challenge any and all corruptions of those ideals. In strong contrast, false prophets were absolutely lethal to Israel, just as a certain type of progressive intellectual is dangerous today. Israel's false prophets had no fundamental allegiance to the covenant, and the effect of their work was to reinforce the corruptions and injustice. They were not merely off course. They were deadly to Israel's continuing existence because they promoted a different view of Israel's character as a people. In the same way, certain progressive public intellectuals in America are dangerous today because they owe an allegiance to a revolution and to views of freedom that differ decisively from those of the American Revolution and its distinctive views of freedom.

The lesson, of course, is that we should never be seduced by the mere repetition of words such as *values, freedom, progress*, and *change*. The question is whose values, what is actually meant by freedom, and how progress is defined and the standard by which it to be judged. The term *change* can be as deceptive as the term *ess*. The modern world has such a bias for change that the term often refers only to bare change and even to change for change's sake. But in a world of change, any kind of change is enough to qualify as "good" and "progressive." And if there is any change at all, we can celebrate the new, downplay any continuity with the old, and ignore any need to justify or assess the change. Is the change for the better or for the worse? That's irrelevant. All that matters is change. Progress is change and change is progress, and that's an end of it.

Utopianism is bloated with such unexamined presumption. For example, Edward Gibbon, author of the eighteenth-century classic *The History of the Decline and Fall of the Roman Empire*, made this famous claim:

> It may be safely presumed that no people, unless the force of nature is changed, will relapse into their original barbarisms. . . . We may therefore acquiesce in the pleasing conclusion that every age of the world has increased, and still increases, the real wealth, the happiness, the knowledge, and perhaps the virtue, of the human race.[11]

Like all good Enlightenment thinkers of his time, Gibbon was sure the glass was getting fuller all the time. After all, reason and the "force of nature" had decreed it, and he had no way to see how the educated, cultured, and highly civilized Germany of Goethe and Kant would become the barbaric Germany of Hitler, Himmler, Heydrich, and Eichmann.

History and the insistent realism of thinkers such as John Gray allow us no such naivety today. Gibbon died in 1794 during the Reign of Terror, which followed the French Revolution, an atrocity that was considered the epitome of evil prior to the Holocaust. The blunt fact was that in both the Reign of Terror and the Holocaust highly educated, prosperous, civilized nations not only "relapsed into barbarism" but exceeded it in the malignancy of their

Clearly, Gibbon's Enlightenment presumption about inevitable progress through "the force of nature" was sadly off the mark. But from the eighteenth century to the 1960s, when the poisonous effect of utopianism had become too disastrous to ignore, the mere incantation of such words as *progress, improvement*, and *amelioration* was enough to inspire confidence and assure the world of the sunny prospect just over the next hilltop.

Today, after a century in which hundreds of millions of people were slaughtered in the name of grandiose ideologies of utopianism, the presumption of this view of progress is under closer scrutiny. Above all, we can see that for all their exaltation of reason, Enlightenment thinkers showed little sense of self-criticism in their philosophy. It would have been far better for Gibbon to have thought critically all along, as playwright Richard Sheridan did in a speech to the House of Commons during the same generation as Gibbon. In criticizing another member of Parliament, he remarked: "He said things that were both true and new; but unfortunately what was true was not new, and what was new was not true."

In both greater and smaller ways the Enlightenment presumption is still alive and well today. All too often there is a double presumption at work. On the one hand, the present is privileged over the past. On the other hand, the future is privileged over the present. Philosopher Martin Heidegger attacked the presumption in the way we automatically privilege the present over the past, referring to it as "the strutting point."

PARADOX

The third hidden tyranny in our modern view of time is paradox. ch is the speed and pressure of time in our world that incessant ge plays havoc with our categories and our conclusions.

Settled convictions, assured judgments, long-held beliefs, age-old traditions, newly trumpeted discoveries, and radical new fashions are all swept away without ceremony in the tornado of change that is modern time. Little wonder that in sphere after sphere we face a harvest of ironies and unintended consequences. Many of our categories, such as left-right, liberal-conservative, and progressive-reactionary have become so tattered and outworn.

In 1939, almost the midnight hour of the twentieth century when Hitler and Stalin stunned the world with news of their Nazi-Soviet Pact, an English wag remarked that "All our Isms are Wasms." His point is even more apt today. Popular categories have been worn out by overuse and distorted beyond recognition by the unsparing speed of time. How else can one explain what we sometimes see of the amiable hollowness of traditionalism, the blind illiberalism of liberalism, or the breathless progressivism of some conservatism?

"The avant-garde is the rear guard" is said today with good reason, for many twenty-first-century liberals have eighteenth-century views of progress, nineteenth-century views of science, and mid-twentieth-century views of facts and objectivity. The problem is not that these positions are dated—the error of chronological snobbery is itself a legacy of modern time—but that they are untrue. The paradox is evident on the conservative side too. Many conservatives, it is said, hate liberals more than they love freedom. But that is only the beginning of the contortions. Above all, many conservatives today are anything but conservativ when it comes to business and the environment. In these ar no one could be more stridently progressive than our h new conservatives.

There will always be differences over all these ideas and terms. But if advanced modern time is not to be even more tyrannical than it need be, we must each be sure what we believe and be clear about our aims. Our freedom and our humanity are at stake and so also is our ability to seize the day and make the most of life.

THE WAY TO SEIZE THE DAY

NINETEEN FORTY-ONE, THE YEAR I happened to be born, has been described as the true midnight hour of the twentieth century. The lights of freedom and democracy appeared to be flickering, Nazi Germany and Imperial Japan seemed invincible, and the diabolical malevolence of "the final solution" was germinating in the dark recesses of Nazi minds. Seventeen million had been killed in the brutal Japanese invasion of China that was launched four years earlier, and where our family lived near Kaifeng, the ancient capital of the Song dynasty, five million people—including my two brothers—died in a terrible famine caused by an army of locusts and the heartless response of General Chiang Kai-shek to his own people. Later in 1949, living in Nanjing, the ancient capital of the magnificent Ming dynasty and later of Nationalist China, my parents and I witnessed the final victory of Lin Bao and the Red Army and the triumph of Chairman Mao and the People's Republic of China.

In short, the horizon of my early years was filled to over flowing with rumors, brutality, crisis, natural disaster, w death, revolution, terror, and history on a grand scale. Hu life seemed cheap, every day was a challenge to survive, and we who did survive seemed to ricochet from day to day and from place to place, with as little sense of control as pinballs in a cheap arcade machine.

I can't say I thought about such weighty matters at the time. I was eight at the climax of the communist revolution when Mao's reign of terror began, but my father—who was fearless—was like an anchor in the storm around us. I certainly thought about such questions later. My brothers had died. Why not me? How can we say we each matter when we are dwarfed by the cosmos, dwarfed by time, dwarfed by events, and dwarfed even by most of the things that are the backdrop of our own lives, such as the size of the state and the number of our fellow humans on the earth at the same time as we are? For some people, of course, the answer is that we don't matter. Once upon a time, Friedrich Nietzsche wrote, "In some isolated corner of the cosmos, poured out shimmeringly into unaccountable solar systems, there was once a star on which clever animals invented knowledge. It was the most arrogant and hypocritical minute of 'world history': but it was only a minute. After nature drew a few breaths, the star grew still with cold, and the clever animals had to die."[1]

Many people today would agree with Nietzsche, but from the Jewish and Christian perspective he was wrong, badly wrong. Nothing could be farther from the Genesis account of creation and the Bible's evaluation of time, history, and our little individual lives. Do we each have value? Is there any meaning to our lives, even in times of conflict and catastrophe? Yes, yes, yes, Jews and Christians cry out together like a trumpet blast. We may not see it now, but there is meaning to life and to the covenantal view of time and history as a whole. There is meaning in each life because we are each significant and history is singular, so we play our part in a larger picture and a longer story whose ending will make sense of it all when it is unveiled.

Nietzsche did not believe in God, and to his credit he refused to trust in any view of life that favored a human perspective for which there was no foundation without God. Life for him had to be seen against the whole of life and the vastness of the cosmos without God and without inherent meaning. There is certainly a paradox in the Bible's view. We may be "creatures of dust," small in size, absurdly dwarfed by history and outnumbered by our fellow creatures, but we are made in the image of God, and "breathed into by the Spirit of God." So we each have momentous worth and significance, and our little lives make glorious sense— even if it is not always apparent to us within the limited horizon of the here and now.

Perhaps because of those turbulent early years, I have always had a passion to make sense of what was happening around me. Like a dog with oversensitive ears, I have always felt the presence and passing of time acutely. Most people, it seems, fit comfortably into their own times like a hand in a glove and find it strange to think of living in any other time—though of course many feel themselves out of step with their times as they grow older. In his last years, C. S. Lewis famously described himself as a "dinosaur." Doubtless the commonsense realism of those who just live and rarely give a thought to time is enviable in many ways.

There are those who wish they had been born in completely different times and somehow always feel out of joint in their own time. The great Austrian statesman Prince Metternich, who lived from 1773 to 1859, felt this deeply. "My life fell into a disgustin historical period. I was born either much too early or much t late; now I actually feel good for nothing. At an earlier per would have enjoyed life, in a future period I could have bee constructive; today I spend my life propping up decaying buildings. I ought to have been born in 1900, thus having before me the twentieth century."[2] Even the apostle Paul himself wrote that he felt like "one born out of due time" (1 Cor 15:8 KJV).

I have never had the unthinking contentment of the first group or the unsettled restlessness of the second, though for me the blend of time and the times has grown to be one of the major themes in life. I have had an electric sense of "the moment" almost as far back as I can remember, and have constantly wondered what it all must mean. We only live once, and time is short, so time throws down a gauntlet at each moment. Do we rise to meet it and seize the moment or not? Life's challenge, as the British king Cymbeline says to his lords in Shakespeare's romance when he hears that the Romans have landed, is to "meet the time as it seeks us."[3] Or in the famous lines of Brutus in Shakespeare's *Julius Caesar* mentioned earlier, there are tides in the affairs of men that must be "taken at the flood."[4]

NOT A MOMENT BUT A WAY OF LIFE

The Bible's idea of carpe diem, "seize the day," or "redeeming the time" is sharply different from the direction to which most people take the ideal—toward the selfish, the short term, and the purely spontaneous. *There is no surer foundation, no stronger propulsion, and no more soaring vision of carpe diem than within the biblical or covenantal view of time.* Yet just as freedom is not "the permission to do what you like" but "the power to do what you hould," so "seizing the day" is far more than the matter of bare oice—Krznaric's "*that* you choose rather than *what* you choose." you choose, how you choose, and what you choose are all nd decisive factors in the Bible's understanding.

As we have seen already, repentance and forgiveness are the key to "redeeming the time" in terms of the past, and notions such as Sabbath and sabbaticals are a key to redeeming the time in terms of the present. But what of redeeming the time in terms of the future, as "Carpe Diem" is usually understood? Seizing the day or redeeming future time is rising to life within a powerful matrix of truths that sets out an entire way of life in which the ideal of carpe diem can come to its highest fruition. God calls us in the flux and flow of time and history, and the gift of being able to seize the day flowers from a way of life that weaves together three principles: "Walk before God," "Read the signs of the times," and "Serve God's purpose in your generation."

WALK BEFORE GOD

Why "walk before God" rather than merely striking out in whatever impromptu acts of faith or whatever unplanned new directions in life may spring to mind? For one thing, creative improvisation is far more than random impulsiveness, a studied effort to flout the past, a passion to shock the bourgeoisie, or a trendy craze to be creatively destructive. The freest and most brilliant creative improvisations, whether in sport, singing, jazz, painting, dancing, politics, or thinking, are not random acts of fancy but the fruit of a genuine mastery of an art. They are born of countless hours of training, practice, and discipline—the celebrated "ten thousand hours" principle through which mastery has become intuitive and there is freedom for the new and creative. St. Francis of Assisi, for example, was often known for his surprising and spontaneous acts, but far from random, they we born of the depth of his deep and daily relationship with J and his care for his fellow humans and God's other creatur

For another thing, the natural and necessary foundation of the life of faith is *walking before God*. What a person says and does, and how they live in daily life are always the best test of what they say they believe and the truest indication of their intentions and motivations. Goethe remarked that "we should try in vain to describe a man's character, but let his acts be collected, and an idea of the character will be presented to us."[5] That may sound obvious, but it is not how many people think about God and faith. Just ask the question, Is there a God, and what is the best way to know him? and most people will answer in terms of philosophy. Western thinking and faith have been heavily influenced by the Greeks, and many people therefore tend naturally to discuss God using philosophy. They think about God and understand faith through philosophical arguments and proofs, using logic and building a case from nature (for example, the famous theistic proofs for God).

Yet the Jewish people have long pointed out that God is introduced in the Bible through history rather than philosophy, and that faithfulness (or reliability and loyalty) is central to the notion of faith. Faith in God is not the conclusion of a syllogism or the last link that completes an intellectual chain of logic. God is known in the Bible through the story of encounters, in experience, in history. The Jews knew God unmistakably because he rescued them from slavery in Egypt, and they saw and experienced his majesty at Mt. Sinai. As the rabbis point out, one might expect the Ten Commandments to be introduced with the words, "I am the LORD your God who created the heavens and the earth." But what God actually said in declaring them was, "I am the LORD your God, who brought you out of the land of Egypt, out of the house of slavery" (Ex 20:2). They knew God unmistakably through his acts in history—the ten plagues, the parting of the Red Sea, the encounter at Mt. Sinai, the provision of water and manna in the wilderness.

This emphasis on the walk of faith is striking in the description of God's call to Abraham. The text in Genesis is very specific about what he is to leave and break away from:

Go forth from your country,
And from your relatives
And from your father's house,
To the land which I will show you. (Gen 12:1)

But it is silent—it says absolutely nothing—about what he is to do when he gets there. All Abraham is told is "Walk before Me, and be blameless" (Gen 17:1). The same was true for the first followers of Jesus. They became "followers of Jesus" or "followers of the Way." The good news the early Christians trumpeted to the world was the story of what God had done and what as firsthand witnesses they had seen with their own eyes and heard with their own ears. But their basic witness was the way they lived it out in their lives—their "walk."

This stress on history rather than philosophy is behind the vast difference between what Pascal described as "the God of Abraham, the God of Isaac, and the God of Jacob," who is not the "god of philosophers and scholars." A truth well-lived outweighs both a truth well-stated and a truth well-argued. A truth well-stated is excellent, but a truth well-lived is priceless. To say that is not to disparage good philosophy. Good philosophy is a matter of "good thinking about thinking," and it is especially crucial for establishing the sort of wisdom common to all human beings as well as for clearing the ground and showing that faith is neither irrational nor foolish as critics claim. But God is primarily know through his actions in history and in the lives of individu rather than through arguments alone.

Above all, the reality of God is better demonstrated in the story of the life, work, death, and resurrection of Jesus than in a thousand arguments about the existence of God. And the credibility of faith shines out more clearly in a life of real faith than in the statement of mere beliefs or the declaration of a creed. A life of faith is the story of the truths Christians believe but are embodied in human form. Each such life adds its support to the voice of the Bible as the grand story of a thousand smaller stories of God's breaking into the experience of human beings in real life. To be sure, words count crucially, propositions matter vitally, and truths about God may and must be stated theologically and accurately, as in the majestic prophecies of Isaiah, the profundity of St. Paul's arguments to the first Christians in Rome, or in the historic creeds of the church. Clarity of faith is essential, loyalty to truth is all-important, and truth claims must always be set out as cogently as possible. But the multilayered reality of truth comes into its own in the visible, audible, and tangible reality of a life lived by faith.

Many implications flow from this point. For example, the reminder and insistence that faith (in Hebrew *emunah*) means faithfulness, loyalty, and trustworthiness, so that apostasy is tantamount to adultery, a violation of love and loyalty and not simply a failure of theological correctness. But one central implication is that the life of faith is a way of living in relationship with God, and not simply a matter of a stated belief. For people of faith, this means that seizing the day is never a sudden impulse or a random act of unplanned inspiration. It is not a whim or short-lived intention like a New Year's resolution. Seizing the day is the creative expression of a seasoned way of life that knows God and is steeped in always seeing time, history, and life "under God," and in living

God's way faithfully before him. "Walking before God," then, is living as God intends us to live, and the essential foundation without which making the most of life is impossible.

IF YOU DON'T GET IT, YOU DON'T GET IT

The second major requirement for seizing the day, redeeming the time, and making the most of life is *discernment of the moment and the hour*. Aware of God, we are aware too of our world and our times. With one hand on the Bible and the other on the newspaper or the Internet, we are called to "read the signs of the times." Both the Hebrew Bible (the Old Testament) and the New Testament are full of examples of discerning the times—or failing to do so. Some are positive and some negative. For many people, the positive examples in the Old Testament are better known and much loved. For instance, some of King David's men from the tribe of Issachar were described as skilled in reading the signs of the times (1 Chron 12:32). Even more famous are the words of Mordecai to his cousin Esther, queen of Persia, "Who knows whether you have not attained royalty for such a time as this?" (Esther 4:14). There are striking negative examples in the Old Testament too, and above all the sobering fact that, with the exception of only two men—Caleb and Joshua—the entire generation that Moses liberated from Egypt failed to make it to the Promised Land. Through one of the gravest incidents of mistrust in Israel's history, second only to the flagrant rebellion over the Golden Calf, an entire generation—as a generation—was judged unworthy of entering the land.

At first glance, the New Testament appears to have more negative examples than positive. The reason is that in all four Gospels the generation Jesus came to simply did not "get" him, including his own disciples for the longest time. In the Gospel of Matthew, for example, Jesus chided the Pharisees and Sadducees because their discernment did not match their weather forecasting. "Do you know how to discern the appearance of the sky, but cannot *discern* the signs of the times?" (Mt 16:3). In a single chapter in Luke's Gospel, Jesus repeatedly hammers on the term "this generation" and declares that their generation was culpable, and that the people of Nineveh and the Queen of Sheba would rise up against them at the Day of Judgment because someone far greater than Jonah or Solomon had appeared to them and they had failed to "get" it (Lk 11:29-32).

Yet unquestionably, the profound depths of the failure to see who Jesus was and what he was about were mirrored most deeply in Jesus' lament over Jerusalem. "He saw the city and wept over it, saying, 'If you had known in this day, even you, the things which make for peace! But now they have been hidden from your eyes . . . because you did not recognize the time of your visitation'" (Luke 19:41-44). Or as another translation puts it, "all because you did not recognize God's moment when it came" (NEB). Remarkably, the suggestion is that Jesus was able to see not simply two aspects of time but three—his own day that was right in front of him, the coming day in AD 70 when the Romans would sack Jerusalem, and a third day, the day that might have been theirs if his generation had responded to him and chosen the way that led to peace.

Does this challenge to discernment mean that "reading the signs of the times" is simple and straightforward? Far from it. The science of weather forecasting has advanced a long way since Jesus accused the Pharisees and Sadducees of hypocrisy, though making sense of history and "reading the signs of the times" is as difficult as ever. But the reason for the widening gap offers us a clue to the way forward. Reinhold Niebuhr put his finger on the problem. There is a marked difference between studying nature and forecasting the weather on the one hand and interpreting history accurately on the other. The difference lies in the role played by the human heart in the two enterprises.

When we study nature, Niebuhr points out, the mind is at the center and the self is at the periphery. So while we will never be other than finite people, we can be at our most objective when we look at nature. But this relationship is reversed when we study history. History is a participant enterprise. All our desires, emotions, prejudices, and interests come into play, consciously or unconsciously. History is all about people, and there are people that we as people dislike, leaders that we mistrust, events that we fear, and outcomes that we long for, even if we are hardly aware of it. So our emotions crowd in and interfere, our blind spots play a part, our minds are pushed to the side, and we are rarely as objective as we think. That is why history itself and our daily newspapers can easily become propaganda and political weapons, again often unconsciously. In short, Niebuhr argues, the problem we face in interpreting history is not a "defect of the mind" but a "corruption of the heart"—which means that eliminating error has to be moral and spiritual, and not purely intellectual.

The Zealots at the time of Jesus did not "get" him because their political views distorted the lenses through which they saw him. Jesus rode in on a donkey, not a war charger, so clearly he could not drive out the Romans and was not the messiah they were looking for. They wanted a "God's hammer," Judas Maccabeus, to free them from the Romans and not a "suffering servant" to free them from their sins. Even Jesus' closest friends James and John did not "get" him at first because they and their mother had ambitions for themselves that were at cross-purposes with what Jesus was calling them to.

Against all such personal or public distortions, we need to apply the correctives of what it means to think Christianly. The fear of the Lord is indeed the beginning of wisdom because it leads to the vantage point and to the humility that enable us to view everything under the aspect of the kingdom, with our selves more firmly in place and out of the center. Then the importance of growing in the fruits of the Spirit comes in, to help correct the biases and corruptions of our hearts we are unaware of. The role of friends is vital too, for "Iron sharpens iron, so one man sharpens another" (Prov 27:17). Which in turn underscores the importance of always being open to correction, for we all often go wrong, we make mistakes, and we need to be set back on the track of the truth. And finally, it is essential that we are led by the direct prompting of God's Spirit, for only the Spirit of God knows the truth of the situation, and he alone can cleanse our muddied lenses and open our eyes to see what is really happening and what God is really doing in our time.

GOD'S PURPOSE IN OUR GENERATION

The third major requirement for seizing the day and following God's call in time and history is *to seek to serve God's purpose in our generation*. King David's men were not simply skilled in reading the signs of the times. They "understood the times, with knowledge of what Israel should do" (1 Chron 12:32). They were not simply pundits, and their knowledge was never for its own sake. What they had come to know through their discernment was to be lived out, and the wiser and more accurate the discernment the more faithful the actions and the lives that flowed from it.

For followers of Jesus, the same thrust is at the heart of the Lord's Prayer, "Your kingdom come. Your will be done, on earth as it is in heaven" (Mt 6:10). God's call is always deeply personal, but it is also always a call to the higher and wider purpose of advancing God's rule on earth. One glorious expression of this aspect of calling in time is the little, almost throwaway description of King David himself, when the apostle Paul remarked, "For David, after he had served the purpose of God in his own generation, fell asleep" (Acts 13:36). There is a surprising tribute there—David served. "Servant leadership" has been reduced to a cliché today, and the contrast with ancient rulers lost. The pyramids and the ziggurats, for instance, were statements in stone, and the top stone stood for the king with the whole weight of the society there to support him. The gods ruled the heavens, the sun ruled the sky, the lions ruled the animal kingdom, and the king ruled his people. But from Moses on, the rulers of Israel were called to be leaders who served. They served both God and their people, and in serving their people, they served God's purpose in their time.

That brief sentence of tribute to David is packed with meaning and lessons. It refers to a significant task, a specific time, and a simple terminus. David, described by God in the same chapter as "a man after my own heart," served God's purpose in his own generation and then left the earth, his task done. But together it adds up to a Jewish and Christian description of carpe diem, seizing the day, redeeming the time, and making the most of our lives—people of faith discerning the times and serving as partners with God to fulfill his will for their times and help to restore the world to what it was intended to be.

Many other points from the Bible's view of time might be considered. For a start, life is a gift, so time is always a matter of stewardship. Especially considering the shortness and fragility of life, both time and money must be spent well. Or again, the Old Testament, for instance, clearly distinguishes between the role of the prophet and the role of the priest in terms of their attitudes to time—prophets being generally concerned with the present or "the future in the present, the end already implicit in the beginning," and priests with the eternal, prophets with the relevant and the spontaneous, priests with the regular and the structured and the ordered.[6] Seizing the day is therefore prophetic at heart. Or again, Jesus put an important emphasis on "dailiness." ("Give us this day our daily bread" [Mt 6:11]; "Sufficient unto the day is the evil thereof" [Mt 6:34 KJV].) Seizing the day is therefore born of a sense of the responsibility of this day's immediacy and the necessity of the hour and our neighbor's need.

Or yet again, St. Paul reminds us that we must have no illusions of perfection in either our thinking or our behavior. Try as we should to read the signs of the times well, we still "see through a glass, darkly" (1 Cor 13:12 KJV). We are not omnipotent or omniscient, so neither our understanding nor our actions will ever be perfect in this life. "Imperfect" will always be written over our understanding and "incomplete" over our actions and our lives. Our best reading of the signs of the times is bound to be flawed. Equally, our best actions will be incomplete, so our true legacy will never be clear until we see God face to face and hear the Master's "Well done" that only he can pronounce.

Until that great day, all our enterprises must be rooted and anchored in humility, remembering that our best judgments and our best efforts will one day be under judgment themselves. But while our days on the earth may be short, our best understanding faulty, and our noblest endeavors often incomplete, we are still to "choose life," seize the day, redeem the time, and seek to serve God's purpose in our time. Then the way we die will be the natural expression of the way we have lived, and both living and dying will demonstrate the faith that has inspired us. Then too, whatever the period of history we are called to live in, arduous or easy, we may join in the ancient Jewish prayer from the time of the Maccabees: "Privileged, O Lord, are we to live in this generation."

5

PROPHETIC UNTIMELINESS

THE TANGLED CRISIS OF THE Western church in the modern world bristles with ironies. For a start, the church that has conformed uncritically to the very world that it helped to create is strenuously working to dig its own grave. Which means that even in countries such as the United States, where the church still represents a large majority of the people, it has less influence on society than tiny minorities that are a fraction of its size. And as the church staggers around dazed and hurt over its rejection, many Christians add insult to their own injury through their fatuous attempts to remain relevant to the modern world in ways that only accelerate their irrelevance.

"The king is dead. Long live the king!" That famous cry that captures the succession from one monarch to another is often applied to time as if the transition were the same—"The past is dead. Long live the future!" But the double twist in thought should alert us to the error. The past is presumed dead and gone, and the present is leapfrogged altogether for the imagined improvement of the future. But while the past is certainly past, it is far from dead. It is hugely powerful in the present, even when the present is reacting vehemently to the past. The past is always present in a person's awareness of self, in their conscious and unconscious memory, in the character they have built through their choices, in their patterns of speaking, and of course in additional ways such as any guilt carried over from misdeeds in the past. As William Faulkner wrote in *Requiem for a Nun*, "The past is never dead. It's not even past."[1]

But if the present should not be privileged over the past, neither should any imagined future, whether desired or dreaded, be privileged over both the present and the past. The past, the present, and the future should never be divided. The three faces of time are one and indivisible. They are one before God, and they are far more intertwined and omnipresent in our lives than we often realize. There is certainly a sense in which the past is no longer, and the future is not yet, but that commonplace distinction is often cited too lightly. As H. Richard Niebuhr noted, the past may be "no longer" but it is "still present," and the future is "not yet" but it is "already present," whether through our hopes, our visions, our excitement, our anxieties, or our fears.[2] The clock may leave two o'clock behind as its hand moves toward three o'clock, but people in time never leave their past selves behind as they move on in life—even if they are born again and grateful to say with the blind man Jesus healed, "Though I was blind, now I see" (Jn 9:25). People of faith should appreciate the past, the present, and the future equally, if appropriately, and they should guard their relationship to all three with vigilance and care. As Niebuhr concluded, "Past, present, and future are dimensions of the active self's time-fullness. They are always with it from the moment it has realized that 'I am I.'"[3]

DISTORTING THE PAST

There are several places where distortions of time are seriously damaging the life and witness of Christians today, but let me focus on three that are especially important—one in connection with the past, one in connection with the present, and one in connection with the future. Together they are crippling the special balance and the rich fruitfulness that the biblical view of time provides. In the covenantal view of time in the Bible, the past is past but a rich treasury for faith and faithful living. There is no daylight at all between the Hebrew Scriptures and the Christian Scriptures in their conviction that memory and history are at the heart of faith. Both Jews and Christians owe their salvation entirely to God—Jews in terms of their national exodus from Egypt and Christians in terms of their personal exodus from lostness, sin, and death. Gratitude for their rescue is therefore foundational to Jewish and Christian trust in and allegiance to God, and memory is gratitude's oxygen just as forgetfulness is its poison. The twin commands to "remember" and "do not forget" are the indispensable bookends of biblical faith. "Judaism is a religion of memory. . . . Memory is a moral tutorial," Rabbi Sacks insists, quoting George Santayana's famous maxim: "Those who cannot remember the past are destined to repeat it."[4]

Remembering like that is never bare memory or mere recall. What is critical for those who remember the past fruitfully is the way they respond to it, for sooner or later an important fork in the road will emerge. There is all the difference, Sacks notes, between "living *with* the past" and "living *in* the past." The former is positive and life-giving, whereas the latter is mere nostalgia, negative, and life-threatening.[5] Today, a key way in which modern people distort the past is through victimhood and hate. Though opposite sounding, they are in fact a weak and a strong form of the same mistaken way of living in the past.

Contrary to the prophets of Enlightenment optimism and their heirs today, evil, injustice, and suffering are rife in the modern world and on a scale that is global and momentous. Beyond all question, today's world is weighed down with victims, the air is heavy with their cries, the ground is soaked with their blood and tears, and our hearts must be fired with passion that is God's passion for justice for the captive, the bullied, and the oppressed. Quite simply, the world of today is overwhelmed with people past counting who have been wounded grievously through the actions or apathy of others, and their blood cries out to heaven.

But that said, to be a victim and to respond through victimhood and victim playing are quite different things. No people on earth can claim to have been victims longer and more often than the Jews. But while the Jews have every reason to respond as victims, they resolutely refuse to play the victim card, and in their refusal they highlight the flaw in today's rage for victim playing (more victimized than thou). Those who *perceive* themselves as victims and respond by *portraying* themselves as victims end by *paralyzing* themselves as victims. The reason is that in seeking to use the past as an instrument of power, victims remain prisoners of their past and never become free. They become prisoners of their own resentment. The Jews, by contrast, look forward, not back. In short, victim playing is disastrous and counterproductive both to the victims and to the victims' society. Homosexuals may complain of homophobia and Muslims of Islamophobia, but Christians who play the victim card and complain of Christophobia have not understood the heart of their own gospel.

If victim playing becomes a distortion of the past through a passive response, hate is an equally dangerous response in an active form. Once again, there is usually no question about the fact of the wrong inflicted. Some genuine, perhaps horrendous, evil has been done—the Nazi extermination of the Jews and the gypsies or the evils of the chattel slavery inflicted on Africans by the Arabs, the British, and the Americans. But in responding to the wrong with hate, the victim turned hater only compounds and perpetuates the problem. Hate spreads the malice (evil aforethought) so that it comes to infect both sides, not just the perpetrator's, and the victims become doubly victims—victimized first by the evil done to them and second by the hate to which they are now a prisoner. For as Sacks notes again, "A people driven by hate are not—cannot be—free. . . . To be free, you have to let go of hate."[6]

But how does hate come in as a problem for Christians now? Too often the accusation that Christians are haters is entirely false. Christians are charged with being hatemongers merely because they disagree with others. In the exploding minefield of today's culture wars, disagreement is often attacked as discrimination and then denounced as bigotry and hate. ("Hate is not a family value," as the bumper sticker protested.) So Jews and Christians who wish to think and live differently from the surrounding culture fall foul of the hate charge—by definition.

Except in rare cases, that charge is neither true nor fair, and the blanket accusation of discrimination and hate degenerates into a serious assault on the right to dissent and to conscientious objection. But the accusation of hate is not where the real problem arises today. The problem is not that Christians are victims of other people's prejudices—Jesus warned his followers to expect that. The problem is that some Christians are becoming unwitting perpetrators themselves—through support of movements that perpetuate hate. In their proper passion for justice, many Christians are supporting movements that claim to combat hate but whose antihate and victim-playing strategies only compound the evil and the hate they claim to fight. There is a world of difference, for example, between Martin Luther King Jr. and Stokely Carmichael and his heirs in today's antiracist movements. But the issue is not just the difference between the two leaders or between the two philosophies of activism—one nonviolent and one more willing to use violence. The deepest difference is between the biblical way of countering evil and the quasi-Marxist way of the secular progressive left and its racial and sexual politics. "Victims" are objects by definition, and they stay so. They may no longer be in slavery, but they remain slaves in their minds. They were dehumanized, and now through victim-playing and hatred they dehumanize themselves and dehumanize others too. "Free men" in contrast are freed men and women who are now subjects and masters of their own responses, with no need to play the victim or to hate anyone. Victim-playing perpetuates victimhood, and hatred corrupts the hater. Both attitudes keep the past alive and maintain its poison, whereas forgiveness frees the victim and cuts off hatred and the past forever.

When the Israelites were freed from Egypt, they had every reason to hate the Egyptians. Who would have judged them for hating the people who had enslaved them so cruelly? Expressed in today's terms, who would have begrudged them reparations for lives and freedoms that could never be recovered? Yet Moses commanded them, "You shall not detest an Egyptian, because you were an alien in his land" (Deut 23:7). Jesus, similarly, called his followers to "Love your enemies, do good to those who hate you, bless those who curse you" (Lk 6:27-28). Freed by God, his followers were called to build a community of free people. They therefore needed to be free from all hate, for hatred poisons society and holds the hater captive as mercilessly as any ancient Pharaoh, Southern overseer, modern tyrant, or sexual predator. Will the United States ever transcend racism and sexism? Certainly not through the ways in which racial and sexual politics are being waged now.

Booker T. Washington exemplifies the way of the gospel in shining contrast with many of today's racial and sexual activists. Freed by Abraham Lincoln from slavery in Franklin County, Virginia, Washington was remarkable for his complete absence of any bitterness. "I resolved," he wrote, "that I would permit no man, no matter what his color might be, to narrow and degrade my soul by making me hate him. . . . I pity from the bottom of my heart any individual who is so unfortunate as to get into the habit of holding race prejudice."[7] In strong contrast, he wrote, there were those then (and there are those today) who make it their business to keep stoking racial wrongs in the public square. "Some of these people do not want the Negro to lose his grievances because they do not want to lose their jobs."[8]

Born in slavery and facing the dark rise of the Ku Klux Klan, Booker T. Washington knew the degradation of slavery all too well and hated it as an institution—as we should hate racism today. But unlike many activists today, he was a man without bitterness. The stark contrast between the spirit of such great African American champions and that of many of today's racial activists is stunning. These great ex-slaves and opponents of slavery knew that freedom that begins in the heart must never issue in hate, whereas activism that is not free in the heart only compounds hate even as it claims to fight hate. Justice pursued with hate leads only to more evil and even greater injustice. To be reconciling and restorative, justice must be pursued with an eye to the possibility of genuine repentance, genuine forgiveness, and genuine reconciliation—and thus with hearts that are freed from bitterness. The past is always present. It is certainly not dead. But forgiveness and reconciliation can draw the poison out of hate so that the past no longer kills the present but liberates it to go forward freely into the future. Through repentance and forgiveness the poison is prevented from spreading. The ball and chain is broken. Reaction need no longer follow action. Even before the end of time, the past can be redeemed in part, with the evil acknowledged and contained.

This point is urgent for countries loaded down with chronic and enduring evils from the past, where the true wrongs need to be righted—such as class divisions in Britain and racism and sexism in America. The prospects for these countries are bleak unless these evils are resolved. The Bible's notion of repentance (*teshuvah* in Hebrew, *metanoia* in Greek) is both radical and strenuous and far deeper than mere appeasement or a formal apology. Fully understood, it contains three elements: admission (the wrongdoer's recognition of having done wrong), confession (the wrongdoer's wider acknowledgment and responsibility for the wrong), and transformation (the demonstration that the wrongdoer would not repeat the wrong, even in the same circumstances, because of significant change in the heart of the wrongdoer). Forgiveness therefore involves a complete change in moral attitude (being truly sorry) as well as a spiritual and social act (coming home to the person, the family, and the community, like the prodigal son from alienation and exile in a far country).

Genuine repentance and forgiveness are radical, practical, and deeply needed today. They both turn on human freedom and choice, and with that freedom they are able to liberate the past and open up a future that is truly different. The irreversible past is no longer the inevitable future. A new day is possible. Without repentance and forgiveness, wrong continues, guilt and resentment mount up, and the result can only be violence, vengeance, victimhood, and the prospect of an endless vendetta in one form or another. But with repentance and forgiveness comes the possibility of reconciliation, and the way is opened to a genuine homecoming for either a person or a nation. Evil acts to alienate, separate, and exile person from person and from family and community, but repentance and forgiveness reconcile and bring them home.

Genuine reconciliation is the most prominent benefit of the Bible's view of tackling injustice, and strikingly, the biblical view of time and providence is a key part of the remedy. The Bible has an unvarnished realism about evil and injustice, but time, providence, and the double freedom of repentance on one side and forgiveness on the other hold the key to a significant containment of evil. In particular, they prevent the past from threatening to ruin the future. Evil and wrong deeds are never other than evil and wrong, and they need to be identified and addressed. Such actions by significant people in a singular history remain evil and unjust. But the evil and the injustice can be contained, and to some extent changed in two significant ways.

First, when wrongdoers repent, they can look back later in time at what they have done, and if they repent, they can recast and cancel their motive for the evil done. The deed remains. It was done and cannot be undone, but the intent is changed. Repentance therefore acts retroactively to separate the motive of the deed from the evil of the result. The deed may be as heinous or harmful as ever, and in the case of many acts, such as murder, the deed remains irreparable. Yet those who repent and confess go on record against themselves. They admit that the act was evil, shoulder the responsibility for it, and recast the motive as wrong and no longer right and justifiable as they originally excused it.

Had they as wrongdoers seen the wrong as they see it now that they repent, they would not have done what they did and they would not do it again. What they said or did was wrong, they admit their guilt and ask for forgiveness. Thus the past is still the past, but in terms of the future it is no longer *fate*. Time and the freedom of repentance (especially when met with the countering freedom of forgiveness) can soften and contain the wrong, and in that limited sense transform it significantly.

Hannah Arendt explored this link between time and forgiveness in *The Human Condition*. We never know the full consequences of our actions, but once they are done, they can never be undone. Wrong acts, even unintentionally misguided acts, can create consequences that close in on us like the relentless severity of Inspector Javert in Victor Hugo's *Les Misérables*. If that were the whole human story and there were no forgiveness, our wrong deeds would bring down on our heads a fate as remorseless as that of the Babylonian stars or Greek fate. Like Sophocles's Oedipus, we would be inescapably doomed, though our fate would be our own responsibility rather than the voice of the oracle at Delphi—"he who acts never quite knows what he is doing, that he always becomes 'guilty' of consequences he never intended or even foresaw, that no matter how disastrous the consequences of his deed, he can never undo it."[9] For most of us, there are so many words we have spoken that we wish we could take back, and sometimes there are deeds we have done from which we could never recover. The words, the deeds, and the damage are done, done, done, and we are doomed, it seems, to live with the broken pieces.

Repentance, forgiveness, and freedom are integrally linked. Repentance and forgiveness are direct expressions of human freedom, just as wrongdoing is, and the freedom of repentance and forgiveness has the power to change the story. Freedom means that things can always be otherwise—they can be other than they are. Determined by the past, "fate" may appear ironclad, and "necessity" may seem natural, logical, irreversible, and inevitable, but their logic can all be cancelled and significantly reversed through repentance and forgiveness. In Arendt's words, forgiveness is "the only reaction which does not merely re-act but acts anew and unexpectedly, unconditioned by the act which provoked it and therefore freeing from its consequences both the one who forgives and the one who is forgiven."[10] When forgiveness breaks into the story, whether God's forgiveness to us or our forgiveness to each other, the cycle of revenge and retaliation is broken.

Second, time helps in another way too. It lends perspective to the deeds of the past and sometimes to the hand of providence that may also become clear. Hindsight often reveals that there are silver linings even among the darkest storm clouds. "Time will explain," as Jane Austen wrote in *Persuasion*. In the book of Genesis, for example, Joseph was able to look back on all that his murderous brothers had intended to do and had done to him, and all that he had suffered as a consequence, including exile, slavery, and prison. Yet he could still say, "You meant evil against me, *but* God meant it for good in order to bring about this present result, to preserve many people alive" (Gen 50:20). His brothers' deeds were still evil, but in light of all the providential consequences that had flowed from their acts, it was easier to forgive the wrongs and thus to contain the original evil and not let the poison spread out through the family and down through the generations.

In the same way, there was no more malignant and malevolent deed in the twentieth century than the diabolical evil of Hitler's "final solution" and the Holocaust that executed it. No amount of time can or should soften that judgment. Yet there is also no question that the vileness of Nazis' evil was linked to the good that resulted in the recognition of the state of Israel and the passing of the Universal Declaration of Human Rights in December 1948. The former, in Jewish eyes, led to "a redemption more astonishing than any other in post-biblical history: the only time a people dispersed for two thousand years has returned to its land to begin its history again as a sovereign power."[11]

One lesson is clear. Calls for justice today should never be considered self-evident and self-justifying. They should be assessed. There are different views of justice and different ways of pursuing it. Christians who stand and salute at the mere mention of the word *justice* are often naive. They can find themselves in movements that perpetuate, rather than solve, the evils. Imagining themselves heirs of the great Hebrew prophets, they become "useful idiots" for the heirs of Karl Marx and other current radical movements. With its remorseless drive for reparations and revenge, the secular pursuit of justice is often resentment fueled and rarely does more than make the injustice insoluble. If the past is not to become a ball and chain for the present, it takes truth, repentance, forgiveness, and reconciliation to keep the past as the past and create an open future of the genuine second chance. The secular pursuit of justice rarely offers such options.

DISTORTING THE PRESENT

The second current distortion of time concerns the distortion of the present through which the present is magnified at the expense of both the past and the future.[12] A clear example is the rage for "generationalism," a way of constantly thinking in terms of discrete generations that warps the present and cuts it off from both the past and the future. Originally, the term *generation* was rooted mostly in biology. Deriving from the Latin word *generare*, it referred to procreation, the act of producing offspring—for example, the famous biblical repetition of "begat." A generation was therefore the time it took for parents to be succeeded by children who had children in their turn. Herodotus describes a generation as thirty-three years, give or take a few years at either end. That meant that there were roughly three or four generations in each century, and—importantly—that all those living at the same time were usually seen as the same generation. In Luke 11, Jesus refers six times to "this generation," and he surely meant all those of any age who were his contemporaries, whether young or old (Lk 11:29, 30, 31, 32, 50, 51).

Our more modern understanding of *generation* grew out of the Enlightenment and put an emphasis on culture as much as biology. It was, therefore, as so often in this period, the product of German studies (philosophers such as Immanuel Kant) and French streets (the French revolutionaries). The Enlightenment put new stress on the possibility of social change as deliberate progress, including the ideal of complete political change through revolution, and on youth as the chosen catalyst for change. This was the era of Young Germany, Young Italy, and later the Young Turks. Importantly too, as youth was elevated, parents and elders were discounted and then discarded as outmoded and redundant as authorities in life.

Generations had always included some acknowledgment of culture, as opposed to biology, but it was usually rather broad—the classical era, or the Augustan, Elizabethan, or Georgian eras. But as the world modernized and change speeded up, the term increasingly referred to age cohorts shaped by the same cultural experiences. Dating became destiny. In the United States in the twentieth century, for example, the Lost Generation (of the First World War) was followed by the Greatest Generation (the Second World War), and then in turn by the Silent Generation (postwar), the Baby Boomers (1946–1964), Generation X (1965–1980), Generation Y or the Millennials (1981–1996), Generation Z (1997–), and so on.

As this narrowing of the generations proceeded apace, some features of the new usage became clear. The emphasis was always on the distinctive features of each generation and therefore the strong differences between them. There was little self-awareness of how the term *generation* was being put to use. And there was almost no discussion of consequences of the new usage and therefore of the stakes for society. Of the features of the new emphasis, the following have become the most important.

First, generation became a key way of describing identity. ("I'm a child of the sixties," "He's a boomer," "She's a millennial.") Thus it takes its place as one more tribal identity in the grand stew of identity politics.

Second, generation became a new form of relativism, added to such other categories as class, race, gender, and religion. ("It's a generational thing. You wouldn't understand.") "Generational truth" therefore joins gender truth, racial truth, and personal truth ("her truth," "his truth") as one more splintering of commonality and objectivity.

Third, generation became a reinforcement of the crisis of authority and the repudiation of the wisdom of experience. A traditional African maxim states, "When an old man dies, a library is burned down," but the essence of generationalism is captured in the 1960s slogans, "Don't trust anyone over thirty!" and "Mistrust authority." Americans should remind themselves why the Romans called their deliberative chamber "the Senate," the name copied by the US Congress. The word came from *senex,* the Latin for "old man." It would take age, maturity, and seasoned judgment to gain the wisdom that running the great republic required.

Fourth, generationalism helps to undermine wider and longer frames of responsibility and solidarity, and therefore puts no checks on such problems as deficit spending (generational theft), environmental degradation (generational irresponsibility), abortion (generational murder), the social security crisis (generational wars), and the careless extinction of other species ("What has the future ever done for us?"). Dostoevsky warned about this problem long ago, "Why should I love my neighbor or posterity, which I shall never see, which will know nothing about me, and which in turn will disappear without leaving any traces or memories?"[13]

Generationalism is therefore a key dimension of what is often called the "tyranny of now" or "short-termism." Such short-term thinking is a key symptom of chronic time slavery, whether expressed through the self-indulgence that only cares about immediate satisfaction or dependency on others that cares only that the next meal will be served to us. Constructive enterprise has a different view of time. It looks beyond the immediate and requires a long-term vision and everything that goes with it: hard work, risk, patience, a willingness to delay gratification, and a capacity to count the days and last the distance. Today's world clearly favors the short term. The financial world thinks in seconds, magazines and the fashion industry think of a season, business leaders think of the next quarter, and politicians think of a term of office. The result is a reinforcement of socialism and a "temporal exhaustion" that disregards the long term and "leaves people out of breath all the time from dealing with the present."[14]

Fifth, generationalism aggravates the breakdown of sustain-ability and of living tradition. Instead of tradition being honored as a matter of safe hands and safe keeping, it becomes the dead hand of the past. In the famous words of G. K. Chesterton and Jaroslav Pelikan, tradition as "the living faith of the dead" be-comes "the dead faith of the living."[15] The Iroquois tribe have a maxim, "What would be good for the next seven generations?" whereas Americans think only of the next business quarter or the next election cycle. Behind traditional attitudes was the simple bet that the combined wisdom of the ages outweighs the best wisdom of any single generation. Every individual human dies, and all human institutions lose energy over time, but living tra-dition is the deepest human way to defeat death and entropy (out-matched of course by the resurrecting and reviving power of God). This idea of intergenerational community lies at the very heart of covenantalism in the Bible. Keep the covenant, renew the covenant, and sustain the covenant and your ancestors live on in you, and you in your children.

Sixth, generationalism parallels radical modern individualism and reinforces the naivety and utopianism of many modern views of human nature. The idea that each generation starts with a new, fresh, clean slate, colored only by its own experiences is blind to a simple fact. "No man is an island, entire of itself" as John Donne insisted, and neither is any generation. Among other things, sin and its consequences link generations with an un-breakable bond and remind us that we are all pieces of a larger continent and links in a longer chain. Like it or not, choices have consequences, and the relationships between the generations are unbreakable at some level. Often for better, sometimes for worse, the old saying was right: "The deepest things passed down in families do not appear in the will." The "sins of the fathers" work their way out in their children and their children's children.

Seventh, generationalism treats the long-term and the far-off as nonexistent and unworthy of consideration. In colonial times there was a legal term *terra nullius* (nobody's land) to justify the colonists' right to colonize, regardless of the indigenous people already there. In the same way, it is said, we are now colonizing the future. Living in our "small here" and "short now," we are treating the future as *tempus nullius* (empty time), regardless of the impact of our actions and ways of life on the life of our descendants.[16]

For all these reasons, generationalism should be a crucial concern to any group of people that depends on a successful handing on of tradition, whether a family, a business, democratic nations such as Britain, Australia, Canada, and the United States, or the Jewish and Christian faiths themselves. Transmission from generation to generation is at the heart of the Christian faith, as it was earlier of Judaism, and it is so because of the character of God himself. God reveals himself as the great "I AM," or more accurately as "I WILL BE WHO I WILL BE," and he adds immediately: "This is My name forever . . . to all generations" (Ex 3:14-15). Simply, ultimately, and forever, God is "He who is." Creator of all else, including space and time, God is "THE LORD GOD, THE ALMIGHTY, WHO WAS, AND IS, AND WHO IS TO COME" (Rev 4:8). Jesus our Lord is "the same yesterday and today and forever" (Heb 13:8).

This truth throbs at the heart of the Jewish and Christian faiths. When Moses renews God's covenant with the people before he dies, he expressly addresses future generations as well as those standing in front of him: "Now not with you alone am I making this covenant and this oath, but both with those who stand here with us today in the presence of the LORD our God and with *those who are not with us here today*" (Deut 29:14-15, emphasis added). There was no greater captain of history in his time than King Nebuchadnezzar, but even he was forced to admit the fleeting frailty of his mighty empire when compared with the Lord, "His kingdom is an everlasting kingdom, / And His dominion is from generation to generation" (Dan 4:3). No wonder the Hebrew psalmist cries out, "Lord, You have been our dwelling place in all generations" (Ps 90:1). This means that our current generational attitudes run directly counter to who we know God to be and directly counter to the biblical view of the generations that in their turn pass before the face of God like armies on parade. But if we have a problem, as we do, the Bible's view of revival also addresses it with hope. Healing is never purely individualistic. It covers the generations too. "He will restore the hearts of the fathers to *their* children and the hearts of the children to their fathers, so that I will not come and smite the land with a curse" (Mal 4:6).

In this grand biblical view, generations are the pulse beats of humanity, and every generation is close to God and responsible to God for its own times, and the transmission from one to another is as crucial to the people of God as it is to humanity at large. Woe betide the family, the nation, or the church that fails to pass on its best and its wisest to the next generation. There are different ways of transmission, of course, and those differences made a difference too. Most of the ancient world commemorated its achievements in monuments and statues, such as the pyramids of Egypt and the statues of Greece and Rome, whereas the Jews relied on stories and human hearts and on families and schooling. The failure of the former was due to the fact that the monuments and statues long outlasted the societies that created them, so all that was left was fit only for museums. The success of the latter

lay in the fact that the way of the habits of the heart, though in-
tangible, has long outlasted the tangible memorials and sustained
a people who have outlived their original neighboring nations
and survived even the most vicious attempts to destroy them.

In Rabbi Sacks's words again, without apology, "What Moses
taught, and what the Jewish people came to discover, is that you
achieve immortality not by building pyramids or statues—but by
*engraving your values on the hearts of your children, and they on
theirs, so that our ancestors live on in us, and we in our children,
and so on until the end of time.*"[17] Long-term thinking always was,
and had to be, a key feature of Jewish thinking. A key question in
his years as Chief Rabbi of Britain was always, "Will we have
Jewish grandchildren?"[18]

Needless to say, there is a huge disparity toward tradition and
transmission within the Christian traditions—between, say,
Orthodoxy and Catholicism on one side and Protestant liberalism
and Evangelicalism on the other. Continuity and change are both
inherent and unavoidable in history, yet the Orthodox and the
Catholics favor the former and Protestant liberals and Evangelicals the latter. The liberals have taken the principle to suicidal
extremes, and there is literally no future for the extremes of
liberal revisionism. But many Evangelicals are unbalanced too
and appear to be foolishly allergic to anything that smells of what
they fear is *traditional* in a negative sense.

Historians say that the sacred music of the Christian church,
such as that of Palestrina, Allegri, and Tallis, is one of the greatest
gifts of the gospel to Western civilization and on a par with the
splendor of the magnificent European cathedrals, such as Chartres
and Lincoln. Yet this rich treasury is an unknown world to many
Evangelicals, whose worship music often draws only from songs

written after 2000 and does not even include the rich heritage of
Celtic Ireland, St. Francis of Assisi, Isaac Watts, Charles Wesley,
and Fanny Crosby. Thank God for magnificent exceptions, such as
the rich, deep hymns of Keith Getty, Stuart Townend, Matt Redman,
and others whose music will join the music of the ages. But much
of the run-of-the-mill renewal songs, which are repeated endlessly and constructed more on rhythm than melody, confine
Evangelicals within a shallow theology, threadbare worship,
fleeting relevance, and historical amnesia. Above all, they de-
prive Evangelicals of the collective praise of Christians down
through the ages as they respond to the grandeur of God in generation after generation. Christians rightly disdain politically
correct thinkers who draw up their skirts in horror at anything
in the past that offends their current sensibilities. Such thinkers
refuse to enter the "chat room of the centuries" that is the three-
thousand-year conversation of our civilization. But in a similar
way, much contemporary Christian music childishly shuts itself
up in the world of post-2000 music and has no idea of the great,
rich "worship service of the centuries" that it is too self-absorbed
to join.

Along with soft preaching and a general rage for relevance
and innovation, such music is another reason why so much
Evangelical church planting does not deliver what it promises. It
resembles a field of quick-growing, fast-disappearing mush-
rooms rather than a long-standing forest of oaks. Again and
again people have regaled me with the church-growth maxim,
"You have to sacrifice one generation to reach the next." But this
turns on a false assumption and leads to the telling fact that the
fatal weakness of Evangelical church growth is succession.
Church growth "success" without succession will always prove a

failure in the end. Will they have Evangelical grandchildren and great-grandchildren?

Put these considerations together and they show why every generation is more flawed than it realizes—and naturally, the next generation knows it and wants to go beyond it. No generation is ever as successful and healthy as it may imagine. It always has flaws that set up the next generation to react against the old one, just as the old one did to their predecessors when they were the younger generation. Every generation must therefore be realistic and humble, and the young just as much as the old. Intergenerational tension is inevitable. The old were all once young, and one day all the young will be old. It does not take long before the vanguard becomes the old guard, the self-professed emergents will have long emerged and disappeared in their turn, and the best and brightest of the golden youth will have aged and died.

For Christians, this appreciation should never lead to weariness or cynicism, but it means that the hope that overcomes it must be solidly anchored in realism. Generations too are touched by life in the fallen world, but their significance in the flow of time and history is vital. The past, the present, and the future are one and indivisible, so the generationalism that privileges the present at the expense of the past and the future is a disaster for the church. Obsessed with their preoccupation with the present, many modern Christians suffer from chronic myopia. But in their shortsightedness they not only forget the past, they also render themselves unprepared for the future, and they lose their hold on their deeper calling in the present. Called to break with the world, Christians are to be fully engaged with every generation but never fully at home with any.

For followers of Jesus, the immediate is never the ultimate, only the interim. Always, we are "resident aliens" in time as well as place. That constant sense of exile and our yearning for our ultimate home is a vital part of immunity to worldliness and to maintaining our Christian distinctiveness and faithfulness along with a forward-thrusting hope.

DISTORTING THE FUTURE

The third current distortion of time concerns the future and centers on the various forms of progressivism mentioned in chapter three. What was said there mostly concerned political progressivism, but the same flaws are at work in religious and theological progressivism. What unites both kinds of progressivism is their beginning and their end. They both start with the naive belief in the Enlightenment creed of constant, automatic, and self-evident improvement, a belief that means that somehow "the newer must be the truer" and "the latest must be the greatest." The Canadian author John Ralston Saul remarked wryly, "It is a general weakness of men delivering ideas that they are able to convince themselves their words represent a break with the past and a new beginning."[19] And they both end in the betrayal of their original convictions.

Owen Barfield called the underlying progressive attitude toward time "chronological snobbery" because the thinking of earlier times is taken to be inferior simply because it is not the thinking of today. C. S. Lewis called it "the fatal serialism" of modern thinking. Just as number 1 always leads to number 2, and 3 always follows 2, so it is thought, the transition from today to tomorrow is always progress from "what is" to "what is better." In short, a position in time overrules the priority of truth. This error over time parallels a similar naivety over size that is a form of "statistical snowballing." ("The bigger, the better" and "the more, the more meaningful." Carl Gustav Jung: "Where the many are, there is security; what the many believe must of course be true.")[20]

Religious progressivism or revisionism has seriously dogged the church since the eighteenth century, first among liberal Protestants but now among liberal and progressive Catholics and liberal and progressive Evangelicals. Indeed, claims to be siding with a future that is inevitable are an early symptom of many a modern heresy and apostasy. Reinhold Niebuhr attacked the underlying malady as the "temptation to capitulate to the characteristic prejudices of an age."[21] The German Protestant theologian Friedrich Schleiermacher was a pioneer when he called his peers to "reach the cultured despisers of the gospel." That goal sounds laudable, but he and those who heeded his call were careless in the way they pursued it. They reached the cultured despisers of the faith and in effect joined them. They reduced the gap between the church and the world to the vanishing point. But then, instead of making it easier for the world to believe the gospel, they made it easier for the church and the world to doubt or disbelieve the faith and thus sold out the faith handed down through the generations in the name of a new and revised form of the faith.

I have described the general process and its flaws in greater detail elsewhere, but it is worth noting the outline of what happens, for the same betrayal happens in similar ways in many different generations and distortion of time is at the heart of it.[22] First, the progressives (or theological liberals or revisionists) *assume* that some aspect of modern life or thinking is superior to what Christians have believed to this point. Second, the progressives *abandon* all that does not fit in with this new assum-

("One can no longer believe this, that, or the other.") Third, the progressives *adapt* whatever remains of the faith to the new assumption. Fourth and finally, the progressives *assimilate* their faith to this new set of ideas. The result may still be "Christian sounding," but the absorption and the betrayal are complete.

There are many examples of such progressive revisionism. Adolf von Harnack, for instance, was a real liberal's liberal, but how was his liberal Protestant Jesus viewed? "The Christ that Harnack sees," one critic said famously, "is only the reflection of a Liberal Protestant face seen at the bottom of a deep well."[23] From Schleiermacher to today's young Evangelical progressives, the story has been repeated again and again, and the outcome is always the same—a betrayal not only of truth but of love, in fact, of "first love," which is why in the Scriptures God views apostasy as adultery.

The worst contemporary forms of revisionisms of faith are mostly the result of capitulating to the seductions of the sexual revolution, which makes the idea of "unfaithfulness" and "apostasy as adultery" even more poignant. Such Christian progressives have been variously described—kissing Judases, defectors, collaborators, fellow travelers, fifth columnists, quislings, turncoats, traitors. The calamitous outcome of their efforts has been similarly assessed—extreme progressive revisionism, one social critic said, becomes "a reduction ad absurdum," a "theological self-disembowelment," a "self-liquidation . . . undertaken with an enthusiasm that verges on the bizarre," and "a bizarre manifestation of intellectual derangement or institutional suicide."[24]

Survey the centuries of progressive endeavors and then assess results. You will be face to face with an unavoidable question: *on earth have so many Christians become so irrelevant when they have tried so hard to be relevant?* After two hundred years of earnest dedication to reinventing the faith and reengineering the church, we are confronted by an embarrassing fact: *Never have Christians pursued relevance more strenuously; never have Christians been more irrelevant.*

My point here is not to target any individual thinkers or writers but simply to show that the entire sad, shabby process starts with a distorted understanding of time. Scientific and technological change may progress dramatically, but faith and ethics do not advance progressively in the same way, and divine revelation is timeless even if our understanding of it has to be adjusted. Yet the irrelevance of the relevance seekers is not the end of the matter. Another curious oddity has become prominent in the Western church over the past two centuries. *Christians who would never fall captive to a major ideology that is alien to the Christian faith leap enthusiastically into the arms of countless passing fashions that are equally alien but miniature ideologies—all under the lure of relevance.*

Fashions have been called "miniature ideologies" or "the lowest form of ideology."[25] The craze for each "new new thing," whether in diets, exercise, clothes, cuisines, or churchmanship, does not last long. But while the reign of each fashion is brief, it extends the royal scepter of social approval to those who adopt it, creates a fortune for those who promote it, sidelines all who disdain it, and demonstrates again and again that modern people have "a need to believe in single-stroke, cure-all solutions."[26]

Relevance itself is not the problem. Properly understood, relevance is a matter of relating to a matter in hand with pertinence and appropriateness. This means that those who define themselves and their lives by the good news of Jesus should be people, most relevant. Relevance is at the heart of the message of Jesus. The gospel is good news, indeed the best news ever. It addresses our human condition appropriately, pertinently, and effectively as nothing else has, does, or can—and in generation after generation, culture after culture, and life after life, all across the world and down through time. It is of course possible that Christians make the gospel irrelevant by shrinking or distorting it in one way or another. But in itself the good news of Jesus is utterly relevant, or it is not the good news it claims to be.

The challenge of relevance in an age that flatters itself as progressive is to be faithful as well as relevant. The answer is to realize the timeliness of untimeliness: to regain the courage of "prophetic untimeliness" and to develop the art of "resistance thinking" and so become followers of Jesus who have the courage to become untimely people despite the mesmerizing lure of the present age and its fixation with the future.

Prophetic untimeliness is a term adapted from the philosopher Friedrich Nietzsche but shaped by the precedent of the Hebrew prophets rather than the German iconoclast. Nietzsche saw that independent thinkers would always be out of step with the conventional wisdom of their generation. Rather than thinkers of their day, caught in the toils of fashion and conformity, they would be thinkers of tomorrow and the day after tomorrow. In short, he wrote in *Untimely Meditations*, they would be "untimely men" or "men out of season." "Their home is not in the present age."[27] They would have the greatest discernment and the most enduring vision born of a different perspective and commitment. In strong contrast to Nietzsche, the north star of the independent thinking of the Hebrew prophets was neither their individual us nor their social stubbornness but the all-decisive authority us says the Lord."

The secret of such prophetic untimeliness is what C. S. Lewis described in a 1945 essay as "resistance thinking."[28] It is a way of thinking that balances the pursuit of relevance, on the one hand, with a tenacious awareness of those elements of the Christian message that don't fit in with any contemporary age, on the other. Emphasize only the natural fit between the gospel and the spirit of our age, and we will have an easy, comfortable gospel that is closer to our age than to the gospel—all answers to human aspirations, for example, and no mention of self-denial and sacrifice.

But emphasize the difficult, the obscure, and even the repellent themes of the gospel, certain that they too are relevant even though we may not see how, and we will remain true to the full gospel. And surprisingly we will be relevant not only to our own generation but also to the next and the next, and the next. C. S. Lewis observed that the same principle holds true in both faith and science: "Progress is made only into resisting material."[29] Resistance thinking, then, is the way of relevance with faithfulness.

Sadly, the word in these paragraphs that causes the most discomfort is *prophetic*. Prophets are the plague of today and perhaps of all time, the Jewish writer Primo Levi declared. He claimed that he didn't believe in prophets even though he came from a heritage of prophets. Doubtless we are right to be wary of false prophets because the modern parade of counterfeits is as long as the list of true ones is short. In many Christian circles, "prophetic" is shorthand for charismatic hunches that are never checked or for any left-wing tirade against the status quo.

But the place of the prophet as one who speaks the word of the Lord is too important to give up, even with the danger of counterfeits. We might distinguish capital *P* "Prophets" from small "prophets." The former are those, like Amos, Hosea, Isaiah,

Jeremiah, who have heard a direct, explicit, supernatural word from God and can legitimately say, "Thus says the Lord." The latter are those who seek to interpret their life and times from a biblical perspective and therefore to read "the signs of the times" with greater or lesser skill, but who never presume the authority and infallibility of "This is the word of the Lord."

In this second and more modest sense, all followers of Jesus are called to be prophets—interpreting events from the perspective of faith and under the aspect of eternity, and always with an eye to what we should *do*, not simply know. As seen with a prophetic eye, the present is not simply a disconnected slice of time. Its significance lies in its unity with the past and the future and the meaning they contribute to it. It may turn out that when we speak in this way, we are sometimes wrong. That is no surprise. On our own we are never more than finite and fallen, so we may get things wrong, and we must always be open to correction. But seeking to read the signs of the times, we have a right and a duty to set things out as we see them under God, though always with humility.

What then is the problem of discernment we are up against in the modern world? It can be stated simply: *Our modern view of relevance has been badly skewed because—once again—our modern fascination with the future is itself the bastard child of the clock culture that is at the heart of the modern world.* We take our modern view of time as natural and self-evident, but it isn't. It's highly unusual, partly helpful, and partly harmful. We therefore need to stand back and view our situation from a wider perspective that understands and appreciates all three faces of time.

I am not suggesting that all progressives and revisionists are ºty of bad faith and aware of their unfaithfulness and dis- ºy. Some of them have indeed drunk the Kool-Aid, others are merely singing for their supper, and still others are deeply sincere and simply trying to do their best. The results, rather than the motives, are for us to judge. What matters for all who seek to be found faithful is a frank recognition of the cost of prophetic untimeliness. A Catch-22 confronts us. True timelessness lies in the untimeliness of rejecting false modern timeliness, but that stance is costly. Seizing our moment depends on our turning from the spurious models of the modern world to seeing the real moment and the real hour as it is seen only under God. But that gain in perspective also brings a gain in pressure. Untimely people find they are swimming upstream and against the current.

False relevance as trendiness is popular, lucrative, and all too easy. But relevance with faithfulness incurs a steep cost. It was said of Edmund Burke, the great Irish statesman and orator, that "Burke was always right, but he was right too soon." Yet that is the least of the problems here. Prophetic untimeliness is out of step with its times in ways that incur a steep cost. As the common experience of whistleblowers shows clearly, and the lives of the prophets and the apostles demonstrate at the highest level, those who pursue true relevance cannot remain sunshine believers.

Prophetic untimeliness requires a careful counting of the cost. It is no accident that the Greek word for "witness" became the word used for "martyr." Those prepared to be witnesses to the good news of Jesus had to count the cost. Plainly they came to the conclusion that even their lives were worth sacrificing for the priceless pearl that is the gospel. It is true that, untimely in their time, they made a stand that is timeless. But nothing can soften the fact that for them and their families, there was a steep cost, and they were re and willing to pay the supreme price.

THE END
IS NOT
THE END

THE GOOD NEWS THAT IS the best news ever is still the best news ever, and all the more clearly so in contrast to history now. Yet in many parts of the West there is an air of discouragement in the church that must be countered firmly. It is born of circumstances, not faith, and while it is not irrational, it is quite unnecessary.

The story of the church in China shows how to look at things in a different way. Four members of my immediate family are buried in China—my Irish grandfather, my aunt, and my two brothers. Educated at Cambridge and trained as a doctor, my grandfather went to China at the end of the nineteenth century and was one of the pioneers of Western medicine in China. He lived and worked in both Beijing, the imperial Manchu capital, and Kaifeng, the eleventh-century capital of the Song dynasty that in its time may have been the largest city in the world. Eventual caring for an imperial soldier so sick that many were afraid to near him, my grandfather took care of him personally but ca typhus and died at the age of fifty-four. Many years later the Red Guards went on a rampage during the Cultural Revo-lution, they tore up and desecrated my grandfather's grave in Beijing, along with those of many foreigners.

My parents were both born in China and educated in Britain, and they worked at the same hospital in Henan that my grand-father had pioneered. Our family was there when World War II broke out, and we soon found ourselves surrounded by the Jap-anese, communist, and Nationalist armies. We were then caught in the terrible famine of 1942–1943, devastated by locusts as well as by the heartlessness of General Chiang Kai-shek, who reserved food for his soldiers rather than caring for his own people. Five million in Henan province died in three months in the appalling conditions, including my two brothers. I nearly died. My mother, who was a doctor, nearly died. And when my parents set out with me to find food and walk to safety, they found themselves in a swirling torrent of refugees estimated to number around ten million.

In other words, my parents' and grandparents' work in China came at great cost. But they were never anything but grateful and filled with joy at the privilege of serving the Chinese people at such a time in their long and celebrated history. After the final communist victory in 1949, my parents were arrested, falsely charged, and kept under house arrest in Nanjing for several years. Eventually, they were released, and they returned to England to tell their story and then resume their work with the Chinese else-where in Asia.

There is no question that my parents felt a deep sadness, disap-
pointment, and concern when they left China—their work that
been cut off abruptly, and the people they left behind were
terrible suffering and persecution under Mao Zedong. But
re never disheartened.

"I am so sorry," I would often hear people say to my father when he spoke at public meetings. "I can't imagine what it must be like to have all that work wasted."

"Wasted?" he would reply. "We were privileged to sow the seed, and what happens now is up to God."

After more than a century and a half of modern mission, there were probably no more than three quarters of one million Christians in China when the communists took over. So the planting had been tough, the brutal systematic persecution of Christians that followed looked dire, and there were many in the West who joined the communists in condemning all missionary work as colonialism. Yet fifty years later, those Chinese Christians had not only stood firm but increased exponentially. There were said to be around one hundred million Christians in China, or more, certainly more than there were Communist Party members, and many members of the Party had themselves become Christians.

So when my father paid his last visit to China in his ninetieth year, he found that Henan province, where we had originally lived, had become the epicenter of the fastest growth of the Christian church in two thousand years. Nanjing, where we lived at the end, had become the world capital for printing Bibles. Accompanying his obituary in the London *Times* was a photo of my father talking to a Chinese man he had led to faith fifty years earlier.

I well remember that when my father returned to England after that last trip, he was simply overjoyed at all he had seen. He was ready to end his days on earth, and die he did, peacefully one night in his sleep. Like Simeon in the Gospel of Luke, his final days on earth were a long and contented *Nunc dimittis* ("Lord, now let your servant depart in peace"). Simeon's famous words cou well have been my father's prayer after that last visit to China. My father had been born in China, grew up in China, married in China, and considered it the privilege of his life to bring the Christian faith to the great nation of China.

The Chinese Revolution of 1949 had been a shattering crisis for the church and a severe test of faith for those who had worked in China. But any hasty assessments or melancholy laments at the time of the Chinese Revolution had been swallowed up in the realization of the long-term outcome. What looks like the end of something is not always the end of the story.

The same would be true of countless moments in the history of the Christian faith. Could the dejected, grieving disciples on the evening of Good Friday see the miracle of Easter Sunday? Could Athanasius, driven into exile yet another time, be sure that orthodoxy would win the day and the world? Could St. Augustine view the shock of the collapse of Rome and of much of the church and foresee how his own vision of the City of God would survive the collapse of the City of Man and contribute to the rise of Christendom centuries later? Again and again the end was not the end, and G. K. Chesterton's famous comment perfectly summed up the outcome: "At least five times . . . the Faith has to all appearances gone to the dogs. In each of these five cases it was the dog that died."[1]

THE END AND THE END

That principle is important today. All across the world the dominant emotion in the global era is fear. With everything interconnected, no one seemingly in charge, events appearing out of control, and individuals feeling overwhelmed by the scale and speed of the problems, fear is real and is far from irrational. Yet for those who trust God and live within covenantal time, the antidote is clear, strong, and bracing. From the beginning to the end of the Hebrew and Christian Scriptures, there is the enduring truth of God's sovereignty and providence. Evil may run rampant, accidents will happen, disappointments and setbacks may dismay the best of us, and at times there may seem to be no meaning to it all. But there is always the relief of the recurring words "But God," and the tirelessly repeated reassurance that is backed by a thousand reasons: "Have no fear."

Our Guinness family motto has long been *Spes mea in Deo est* (My hope is in God). But all whose confidence is in God can rest in the majesty of the truth: *God is greater than all, and God may be trusted in all situations. Have faith in God. Have no fear.*

But what is the remedy for the widespread discouragement in the West—whether in response to the sorry state of Western civilization itself or the dismal condition of the faith that more than any other shaped the West? Grounds for discouragement seem as solid as the grounds for fear, and realism, it would seem, means siding with the pessimists. Enemies and critics of both the West and the Western church are posting their obituaries with glee, and droves of former believers, we are told, are swimming away from what they see as a sinking ship. What no persecutor in two thousand years has been able to do, the advanced modern world has done without a sword, prison cell, or firing squad. Having helped give rise to the advanced modern world, the Christian church seems to be caving in to the world that it helped to create. The church has become its own gravedigger. Modernity, it seems, has won. The church appears to have met its match. The Christian era, it is said, is dead and gone, and the Christian faith is scor as yesterday's faith.

Needless to say, the Bible's enduring reassurance still rings out, "Have no fear." But somehow the discouraged are not encouraged. Is the refrain only an insurance clause that guarantees safe passage for the remnant through the turbulence of the end times? Or is there more to faith than that? Is there solid ground from which Christians may look the challenges of today in the white of the eye and tackle them with confidence? There are in fact numerous truths to buttress the reassurance of faith, and numerous points to offset the potential discouragement.

Times of historical disaster, such as the collapse of the Roman Empire, are always beneficial to the church in the long run. For one thing, they shatter long-unquestioned and idolatrous confusions such the reigning forms of God and government, religion, and civilization. They also tear down the foolish pretention that any of our political systems (such as democracy or socialism) are the culmination and final destiny of history ("the end of history"). For another thing, times of historical disaster open up possibilities that times of power and prosperity have stifled, if unwittingly. God's truth is always richer and more profound than any generation's understanding of it. So the truth that any generation has overlooked, believing in its myopic pride that it knows the full truth, lies in the ground like an unwatered seed ready to spring to life like the blooming of a desert in the spring rains. For yet another thing, times of historical disaster are often the direct inspiration for new and profound insights, such as St. Augustine's portrayal of the City of God and the City of Man. Augustine's vision, as Reinhold Niebuhr remarked wryly, was far more profound than the views of "Constantine's clerical courtiers who reded the stability of Rome as the proof of the truth of the ian faith."[2]

There is no inevitability in history, of course, and the open-endedness of freedom includes the possibility that faith may be stamped out altogether in one part of the earth or another. Jesus himself warned, "When the Son of Man comes, will He find faith on the earth?" (Lk 18:8). But one truth that is often forgotten today is an antidote that is particularly apt for the crisis of our time and a truth that is part and parcel of the covenantal perspective on time: *The end is not the end.*

Stated more carefully, the idea of *end* is understood in two different ways in the Bible and within the Jewish and Christian view of history. The two meanings are completely different, but they must never be divorced, and their relationship is crucial for faith in dark times. "End" in the Bible is sometimes seen as *finis*, in the Latin sense of conclusion, full stop, period, or ending, but the Bible also sees "end" as *telos*, in the Greek sense of goal, purpose, culmination, or climax. Both "end" as conclusion and as climax and culmination are always at work in history, and as much so today as ever. We must remember both, appreciate how they are linked, and live our lives with a firm grasp of both truths.

Viewed according to the first sense, endings are a matter of the course of nature and therefore a matter of plain realism for Jews and Christians. There is no end to our endings, and there never will be while time in a fallen world still lasts. For a start, there are always natural endings in a fallen world. Each day ends and the night falls, just as summer ends and the leaves fall. Just so, all that is new grows old; all that is successful fails; all who are young will age; and all who are human will breathe their las even the Methuselahs of the past and the would-be Methusela of the Silicon Valley future. In the same way, all stories en businesses end, all eras end, and all civilizations end. *T fugit* (time flies); *memento mori* (remember you will die), "This too shall pass." "No man ever steps in the same river twice" (Heraclitus). "Time, like an ever rolling stream, bears all its sons away" (Isaac Watts). Call it the cycles and seasons of nature, call it entropy and the second law of thermodynamics, call it Father Time with his sickle, or call it the fruit of the passing of time and the presence of sin in a fallen world. "In the end," everything ends.

Endings in this first sense are not just a matter of natural realism but of moral realism too. Beyond the natural and inevitable endings of the cyclical nature of time, there are endings that are premature and quite unnecessary—endings that are morally deserved that people bring down on their own heads by their own wrong behavior unnecessarily. The Hebrew prophet Amos, for example, delivered a stern and stunning verdict from God to his contemporaries in the eighth century BC: "The end has come for My people Israel. I will spare them no longer" (Amos 8:2). Crucially, there were no natural reasons for Israel to decline at that time. On a purely historical level, the northern kingdom of Israel was at the height of its power and prosperity; the resurgence of Assyrian power was some years off; and from a directly theological viewpoint the people were only enjoying the land that God himself had promised to Abraham and had given to their ancestors. In other words, viewed from a purely secular perspective, Israel's end was quite unnecessary.

Yet neither the divine promises of the past nor the natural and secular factors of the present were the whole story. What decided ~rael's fate and hastened Israel's end was Israel's disregard for ʒ in the form of its brazen injustice, the brutal and callous ⸱ment of the weak and the poor. For this, there was no re- for morally speaking, there is an appointed end for all evil, and for evil among God's people most of all. Israel's judgment was exile, and Israel's end was its disappearance from history as the ten lost tribes. The end of history as Israel was about to experience it at that moment was explicitly Israel's own direct fault. Sadly, the same appears to be true for the American republic at the moment. If there is no repentance and turnabout, Americans seem intent on bringing down God's judgment and the world's opprobrium on their own heads through their own willful behavior.

In the world as we know it, there is simply no escape from one or the other of these two forms of *end* as ending. If that were the whole story, the emphasis would lead to weariness, cynicism, or despair, but in the Bible that emphasis is not the whole story. As Reinhold Niebuhr declares, "Against such despair the Christian faith insists that the end as Finis is not identical with the end as Telos."[3] In and through each end as ending (*finis*) a higher end (*telos*) is being worked out. Under God, every ending therefore carries a continuing, everything old contains some foretaste of something new, and every failure carries the seeds of a better, higher, and more glorious success—in short, under providence covenantal time leads an irresistible progression toward the higher purpose that only God knows and only God can bring about. The City of Man will always collapse, in one version after another, but the City of God endures.

Just as the apparent *finis* of the cross led to the startling *telos* of the resurrection, so the apocalypse of the end times will one day lead to the restoration of the messianic age. That is why "the gates of hell" (the very centers of the planning and decisions c the forces of darkness) will never prevail against the chu Thus in our own far less significant day, we may be sure that looks to us like the end as endings (*finis*)—the "collapse" church, the "end" of Christendom, the "decline" of the West, or whatever—is in fact moving toward God's end and his momentous and inspiring purposes in history (*telos*). Our task, then, is to look at the end as *finis* with realism and to work and wait for the end as *telos* with hope. Through such trust in God and partnering with his purposes, we can serve God's higher end even in our endings— and even when that higher end is far beyond our sight and quite beyond our ability to bring it about. Work done faithfully and lives lived trustingly are never in vain.

Unquestionably there are many signs of the end as an ending (*finis*) today. The world's lead society is experiencing its gravest crisis since the Civil War, the Western world is in decline, the search for a New World Order is faltering, the church in the West is reeling from assaults from the outside and crises and betrayals from the inside, the worldwide church is suffering unprecedented persecution, and the agenda for humanity in the global era is overloaded with unprecedented crises today and the prospect of even more unprecedented crises tomorrow. And we all have our own personal and family crises too.

Yet all such trends demonstrate only the end as conclusion (*finis*), not the end as climax and culmination (*telos*). Focus only on half the truth and it would be all too easy to grow discouraged and give up. But remember the other half and the present becomes the moment for people of faith to show the difference that faith makes. For followers of Jesus, the end is not the end. Faith should never grow discouraged. Faith should always be encouraged through its hope. That is how in times of darkness, may, and discouragement, and even in periods of violence, death, and chaos, the message of the prophet rings out "the righteous will live by his faith" (Hab 2:4). There are no more realistic faiths than Judaism and the Christian faith, but Jews and Christians live with an undimmed hope even in the darkest hour.

LONG-TERM THINKING

For those who live and act within covenantal time, two immensely practical implications flow from this principle. First, it means that Jewish and Christian thinking is long-term in its thinking, incremental in its actions, and nonhumanist in its confidence. Both faith and hope therefore require patience and perseverance. To partner with God and serve his purposes in the world assumes and requires change, but whether the change is personal and individual or social and political, change takes time because changing the heart is essential. Thus covenantal time helps us avoid two equal and opposite errors, the "all-at-oncers" and the "never-neverers."

The all-at-oncers, or the impatient hotheads, are those who want everything and all at once and therefore take things into their own hands and do whatever it takes—raw, unprincipled power—to achieve their goals in their time. The utopian secular revolutions of 1789, 1917, and 1949 and their reigns of terror are striking examples of this extreme, but there have been religious versions too—*millenarians* of all sorts have rashly imagined that through their end-of-history dreams they were bringing history to an early and glorious conclusion. The never-neverers are those who were once equally passionate and impatient but who gave up hope. They insisted on an achievable, visible, here-and-now form of justice, and then, when they realized that what they desired was impossible, they despaired of everything.

History is replete with examples and warnings of the import of patience over incremental change, starting with the story exodus from Egypt. Liberation was one thing, liberty another. It took only one day for God to get Israel out of Egypt, but it took forty years and more for God to get Egypt out of Israel. Freedom can become the greatest enemy of freedom because there is a certain tyranny in freedom and a certain freedom even in tyranny. Instead of the hard work of freedom and the challenge of responsibility and discipline, we can escape into a nostalgic illusion that twists freedom into slavery (Freedom is much harder than we thought) and slavery into freedom (Slavery is not nearly as bad as we thought). How else could the staggering outcome happen that the leaders of the rebellion against Moses came to describe Egypt, the land of bondage, as "a land flowing with milk and honey," which earlier was the description of the Promised Land? (Num 16:13).

Change takes time. Growth takes time. Freedom takes time. The habits of the heart that form character take time. Reform takes time. Establishing justice takes time. Transmission from one generation to the next takes time. And above all, the final hope of freedom and justice achieved for all takes time. Little by little, inch by inch, day by day, and moment by moment may translate into vast distances and unbelievable transformations. And all too often, hasty assessments and premature conclusions are wrong. We live in an instant society, but the ten thousand hours principle applies to many of the things we most value in life—though the real number should probably be twenty thousand or thirty thousand hours. Like football, piano playing, or ballet dancing, many of life's greatest achievements require dedication, patience, and perseverance if the skill is to become second nature and the virtue a habit of the heart. Our thinking, then, must be long-term thinking, supported by slow and daily incremental growth and improvement, which must be undeterred by the impressions and contradic- of any immediate moment or any interim stage.

ONLY WHEN HE COMES

The second implication is that our partnering with God is real but always reliant on God for the final outcome. Both the Jewish and Christian faiths regard responsibility as the key to charting a course between the two extremes of autonomy and dependency, but responsibility is not self-reliance. Both faiths are unashamedly nonhumanist faiths, and their contrast with optimistic humanism is starkly clear. Humbly, we know that faith in God and its great vision of life are not all up to us. Knowing God is not up to us, but we thank God he reveals himself to us. Salvation is not up to us, but we thank God he rescues and redeems us. Similarly, the end of history is not up to us, and we thank God for that great day when his Messiah will come, the one who will bring the forces of history to the climax he has had in mind all along. There is a promised time as well as a promised land. (On that great day, the only question dividing Jews and Christians, as a Jewish friend says, will be to welcome the Messiah together, and then ask him whether his coming is his first or his second.)

The term *apocalyptic* has become a synonym for catastrophic, but its real meaning is not catastrophe but "unveiling." The catastrophic element will certainly be present at the end times, because the Bible warns realistically that, contrary to the Enlightenment creed of steady improvement, the forces of diabolical evil will persist and even rise to a horrifying crescendo toward the end of history—the "final evil." But that same catastrophic climax will end in both victory and a dramatic unveiling. It will be the moment when the whole world will marvel as they see God unveil the meaning of history and the cosmic purposes that he has been working toward from the beginning.

Once again the biblical view of time shines through brightly. As ever, time is a key to meaning, and all three faces of time are important. The past is always in some way the key to the future because who we have become through our choices will help determine the future we choose and how we respond to the future that confronts us, whether we choose it or not. But in a far greater way the future will always be the key to the past. The past is critical because of our choices and their consequences, but the future will be even more critical because of the Messiah's coming and the great unveiling of the meaning of history at the end of history.

"Time will explain," Jane Austen wrote in *Persuasion*, and Søren Kierkegaard was right that "life can only be understood backwards, but it must be lived forwards."[4] Only the perspectives of time allow us to distinguish the trivial from the important, the passing from the permanent, and the random from the significant. Only when we look back can we connect the dots and make some sense of the story line that is the script of our lives. Yet if that is true in a small way of our individual lives and true of the generation we live in, how much more will it be true of history in the full sweep of its entirety.

While we are still within the bounds of history itself, no present moment for anyone anywhere at any time—not even for the most brilliant and diligent historian—will ever throw enough light on the past to explain it to our full satisfaction. Our understanding will always be incomplete. We are not omnipotent, and we are not omniscient about the past or the present or the future. We still always see only "through a glass darkly." History as the remembered past, which itself is only a tiny part of the full past, raises too many questions. History is bursting with puzzles, contradictions, non sequiturs, dilemmas, loose ends, and of course profound evils. It is too much for even the greatest historian or

philosopher to resolve. But in the light of the great unveiling of
the nonhumanist future ushered in by the Messiah, all questions
will be resolved and all conundrums explained, just as all books
will be balanced and all tears will be wiped away. Every part of
the sad, shameful, sometimes painful, and often-confusing past,
burdened with its evils and its enigmas, will be illuminated and
resolved by the all-transforming future that is unveiled when the
Messiah returns. Time will explain, and time will be explained
at the great unveiling that is the final apocalypse.

After the failure of the rebellion of Scotland's Bonnie Prince
Charlie in 1745, it was impossible for his supporters to toast him
openly, for all their devotion. Instead, they would raise their
glasses "To the King!" as if to the English King George II, and then
pass their toast over a glass of water. They were silently toasting
their king who was "over the water" in France. With even deeper
devotion and with infinitely more solid grounds for confidence,
Christians who celebrate the Great Thanksgiving that is the
Service of Holy Communion look back with gratitude to all that
our King Jesus did through his victory on the cross and then look
forward too with hope—"until he comes."

"Next year in Jerusalem," the Jews say. "Until he comes," Christians declare. Until that great day arrives, we live by faith, with
hope—trusting, obeying, working, looking back with gratitude,
and looking forward with hope. In larger and smaller ways it is
up to us to seize each day and redeem the time we have in our
stay on earth, partners and coauthors with God. But the grand,
final, ultimate carpe diem is in God's hands, not ours. One day, the
day that is the end of all days, God will seize the day as only God
can. He will seize time and history in an ultimate way and reveal
his meaning for humanity, for the earth, and for the universe.
Little wonder that all ends as endings, and even our lives' fir

end, death, will then be swallowed up by God's *great end* that is the climax and culmination of time and history.

Jews like to tell the story of Napoleon passing a synagogue on a fast day and hearing the loud sounds of lament. "What are the Jews crying for?" he asked one of his officers.

"For Jerusalem," the soldier replied.

"How long ago did they lose it?"

"More than 1,700 years."

"A people who can mourn for Jerusalem for so long will one day have it restored to them," the French emperor remarked.[5]

Despite the horrors of their vicious persecution, global scattering, and two-thousand-year exile from their homeland, the Jewish people never gave up hope, and neither will followers of Jesus. Remembering is completely different from nostalgia, and hope is not the same as "hoping against hope." The confident hope that longs and watches for the City of God has been given assurance, so it is sure of its final vindication. Faith's passionate question as it feels the pain of the contradictory and the unresolved, is often, "How long, O Lord?" But its constant and urgent prayer is always, "Come quickly, Lord Jesus."

At the end of time there will be an end that rescues and redeems the past, reversing all previous endings and ushering in a future that to the present is as yet unimaginable. Doubtless our prayers until then will be more urgent and heartfelt at certain times than others, but always our sense of time past and time present will climax in our anticipation of time future. There is no time to be wasted in endless excusing of the past or idle speculation about the future and the legacy of our lives. Seizing the day today, we look back to the first coming of our Lord, and we then raise our glasses to drink to his second coming, the return of our ng from "over the water of time." "Come, Lord Jesus. Come."

CONCLUSION

Choose Life

IN HIS FIRST BOOK, *The Birth of Tragedy*, Nietzsche tells the ancient story of King Midas hunting in the forest for Dionysus's companion, the wise Silenus. Capturing him at last, he asked him what was "the best and most desirable of all things for man." At first the demigod refused to answer, but urged on by the king, Silenus at last gave a shrill laugh and said, "Oh, wretched ephemeral race, children of chance and misery, why do you compel me to tell what it were most expedient for you not to hear? What is best of all is beyond your reach forever: not to be born, not to *be*, to be *nothing*. But the second best for you is—quickly to die."[1] Nietzsche was echoing the words of the chorus in Sophocles's last play, *Oedipus at Colonus*, "Not to be born is best when all is reckoned in, but once a man has seen the light the next best thing, by far, is to go back where he came from, quickly as he can."[2] A familiar Greek adage expressed the same point bluntly: "Call no man happy until he is dead."

The leaders, citizens, and nations of the advanced modern world should ponder Nietzsche's story, for the culture of death is spreading slowly and remorselessly in our time. Death in video games, death in rap music, death in action films, arms dealings, murders, massacres, killing fields, terrorism, abortions, suicides, euthanasia, drone strikes, long-range missile retaliation, robotic AI warriors, an accelerating arms race in space—together, the brutal arm of violence and the shadow of death are stalking the earth. Clearly, the advanced modern world has chosen to beckon the angel of death and plant the skull and bones firmly at the center of its way of life.

With that colossus of darkness glowering over us, there is little chance that those who strive for the carpe diem ideal today will be noted for their altruism and sunny benevolence. In the world that is coming, the impulse toward seizing the day is far more likely to be twisted into acts of selfishness, defiance, and despair. "Those whom the gods love die young," as the Greeks said, so we better get on with it. The altruistic, the benevolent, and the long-term are for the birds. All too often *carpe diem* will be the motto of the rich, the powerful, and the greedy, and it will come down in practice to "Grab it while you can." In shining contrast to this specter, the call of God throughout the Bible and the promise of the Jewish and Christian faiths is clear: "Choose life in order that you may live" (Deut 30:19). Or in the words of Jesus, "I have come that they may have life, and have it to the full" (Jn 10:10 NIV).

Those with the greatest view of time are those best able to use and enjoy the time they have. Life is short, but we are called to rise to our full potential, making the most of it and seizing each day. Within the biblical view of time and history, life offers meaning and opens prospects whose significance far outstrips its shortness. Time is more than cyclical, and its linear progression forms a story in which we come to play a significant and responsible part. History is singular and we are significant, so all that we are and all that we do is consequential. We leave our marks upon the face of time, and our efforts are not in vain. The world has gone wrong, evil and injustice are everywhere, but God invites us to be coauthors of our own lives and partners with him in the wider global reconciliation, repair, and restoration that are underway. So as we strive for freedom and justice in human affairs, we care for our neighbors as well as ourselves. The hope of all that is coming gives strength to what we are doing, just as what we are doing will be a sign of all that we believe is coming.

Our little lives may be incomplete, our grandest visions may be unfulfilled, and our best actions may seem no more than small and inconsequential. But for people of faith who are visionary "dreamers of the day," our actions into time always look beyond the horizon of history to that great day when the widespread ruins of all the recurring versions of the City of Man will be eclipsed by the splendor of the City of God.

In the meantime, let us *seize the day*, this day and every day, and seize the day fully, confidently, and hopefully—but not as self-celebrating, grandstanding minigods on the earth. Let us seize the day humbly as we walk before God, endeavoring to read the signs of the times, seeking always to serve God's purposes in our generation, and working together with all who place their hope in the great messianic Day of the Lord that is coming.

For only when that day arrives will the vast mystery of time and the long-running puzzles of history reveal their true meaning and show us the destination toward which they were moving all along. Only then will the time have come when all "ends" that are endings, including our final enemy, death, will be swallowed up by the crescendo of God's great end. Only then will we know God's full purpose for each of us, for the very planet we live on, and even for the wonder of the cosmos itself. And only then will our will to meaning and our will to freedom be swept up in the far greater will to worship and to love the One at the center of it all.

Until then, we walk on faithfully and fearlessly, day after day, pilgrims across the reaches of time, but traveling always on what we know is the long journey home to our Father.

O God Our Help in Ages Past

O God, our help in ages past,
Our hope for years to come,
Our shelter from the stormy blast,
And our eternal home.

Under the shadow of Thy throne
Thy saints have dwelt secure;
Sufficient is thine arm alone,
And our defense is sure.

Before the hills in order stood,
Or earth received her frame,
From everlasting Thou art God,
To endless years the same. . . .

A thousand ages in thy sight
Are like an evening gone;
Short as the watch that ends the night
Before the rising sun.

Time, like an ever-rolling stream,
Bears all our years away;
They fly, forgotten as a dream,
Dies at the opening day. . . .

O God, our help in ages past,
Our hope for years to come,
Be Thou our guide while life shall last,
And our eternal home.

Isaac Watts, 1719

NOTES

INTRODUCTION

[1]William Shakespeare, *King Lear*, act 5, scene 3.

[2]Leo Tolstoy, *A Confession and Other Religious Writings* (London: Penguin, 1987), 35.

[3]Leo Tolstoy, *The Death of Ivan Ilyich* (Jerusalem: Minerva, 2018), 91.

[4]Abraham Joshua Heschel, *The Sabbath: Its Meaning for Modern Man* (New York: Farrar, Strauss and Giroux, 2005), 98.

[5]Claire Tomalin, *Thomas Hardy: The Time-Torn Man* (London: Penguin, 2006).

[6]Roman Krznaric, *Carpe Diem Regained* (London: Unbound, 2018).

[7]John Keating, *Dead Poets Society*, quoted in Krznaric, *Carpe Diem Regained*, 13.

[8]Krznaric, *Carpe Diem Regained*, 10.

1. SINGULAR, SIGNIFICANT, AND SPECIAL

[1]Augustine, *Confessions*, bk. 1, chap. 14.

[2]Jim Holt, *When Einstein Walked with Gödel* (New York: Farrar, Strauss and Giroux, 2018), 19.

[3]Mircea Eliade, *Cosmos and History* (New York: Harper & Row, 1969), 139.

[4]Aristotle, *De generatione et corruption*, 33.6b.

[5]William Shakespeare, *As You Like It*, act 2, scene 7.

[6]Arthur Schopenhauer, *Parerga and Paralipomena: Short Philosophical Essays*, trans. E. F. J. Payne (Oxford: Clarendon Press, 2001), 2:393.

[7]William Shakespeare, *Macbeth*, act 5, scene 5.

[8]Paul Johnson, *A History of the Jews* (New York: Harper and Row, 1987), 2.

[9]Blaise Pascal, *Pensées*, trans. A. J. Krailsheimer (London: Penguin, 1995), 285.

[10]Abraham Joshua Heschel, *The Prophets* (New York: Harper Perennial, 2001), xviii.

[11]Reinhold Niebuhr, *Faith and History: A Comparison of Christian and Modern Views of History* (New York: Charles Scribner, 1949), 19.

[12]Pascal, *Pensées*, 434.

[13]David Brooks, "The Cruelty of Call-Out Culture," *New York Times*, January 14, 2019.

[14]Yuval Noah Harari, *Homo Deus: A Brief History of Tomorrow* (London: Harper Collins, 2017), 43.

[15]C. S. Lewis, *The Abolition of Man* (Las Vegas: Lits, 2010), 36.

[16]Nick Bostrom, *Superintelligence: Paths, Dangers, Strategies* (Oxford: Oxford University Press, 2014), 5.

[17]William Shakespeare, *Hamlet*, act 5, scene 2.

[18]Rabbi Tarfon, quoted in Jonathan Sacks, *Covenant & Conversation—Numbers: The Wilderness Years* (New Milford, CT: Maggid Books, 2017), 241.

[19]Abraham Joshua Heschel, *The Sabbath: Its Meaning for Modern Man* (New York: Farrar, Strauss and Giroux, 2005), 7.

[20]Jonathan Sacks, *Haggada: Collected Essays on Pesach* (New Milford, CT: Maggid Books, 2013), 32-33.

[21]Jonathan Sacks, *Ceremony & Celebration: Introduction to the Holidays* (New Milford CT: Maggid Books, 2017), 217.

[22]William Shakespeare, *Julius Caesar*, act 4, scene 3.

[23]Bertrand Russell, quoted in John Gray, *Seven Types of Atheism* (London: Allen Lane, 2018), 42.

[24]Bertrand Russell, quoted in Niebuhr, *Faith and History*, 87.

[25]Lewis Mumford, *Technics and Civilization* (Chicago: University of Chicago Press, 2010), 435.

[26]Joseph Proudhon, quoted in Niebuhr, *Faith and History*, 80.

[27]Immanuel Kant and Arthur Schopenhauer, quoted in Sacks, *Haggada*, 47.

[28]Niebuhr, *Faith and History*, 14.

[29]Max Tegmark, *Life 3.0: Being Human in the Age of Artificial Intelligence* (New York: Vintage Books, 2019), 22.

[30]Gray, *Seven Types of Atheism*, 1.

[31]Gray, *Seven Types of Atheism*, 58.

[32]Milan Kundera, *The Unbearable Lightness of Being* (New York: HarperPerennial, 2009), 8.

[33]Joseph Heller, *Good as Gold* (New York: Simon & Schuster, 1999), 72.

[34]John Berger, *Keeping a Rendezvous* (New York: Vintage International, 1992), 29-31.

2. SURVIVAL OF THE FASTEST

[1]Seneca, quoted in Alan Burdick, *Why Time Flies: A Mostly Scientific Investigation* (New York: Simon & Schuster, 2017), 2.

[2]Burdick, *Why Time Flies*, 5.

3. THE HIDDEN TYRANNY OF TIME

[1]John Stuart Mill, quoted in John Gray, *Seven Types of Atheism* (London: Allen Lane, 2018), 91.

[2]Gray, *Seven Types of Atheism*, 82.

[3]G. K. Chesterton, *Heretics* (Mineola, NY: Dover, 2006), 14.

[4]T. S. Eliot, *The Rock* (London: Faber & Faber, 1934), 51.

[5]Gray, *Seven Types of Atheism*, 24.

[6]Gray, *Seven Types of Atheism*, 28.

[7]Henry David Thoreau, quoted in Martin Luther King Jr., sermon at Temple Israel at Hollywood, February 26, 1965, www.american rhetoric.com/speeches/mlktempleisraelhollywood.htm.

[8]Gray, *Seven Types of Atheism*, 28.

[9]Gray, *Seven Types of Atheism*, 95.

[10]Dean Acheson, quoted in Erik von Kuenelt-Leddihn, *The Intelligent American's Guide to Europe* (New Rochelle, NY: Arlington House, 1979), 407.

[11]Edward Gibbon, *The History of the Decline and Fall of the Roman Empire*, vol. 5 (London: Harper and Bros., 1837), 614.

4. THE WAY TO SEIZE THE DAY

[1]Friedrich Nietzsche, unpublished essay "On Truth and Lie in a Morally-Disengaged Sense," in Robert Wicks, *Nietzsche* (Oxford: One World Books, 2002).

[2]Klemens von Metternich, *Aus Metternichs nachgelassenen Papieren*, ed. Prince Richard Metternich-Wineburg (Vienna: Wilhelm Braumüller, 1881), 3.348 (no. 442).

[3]William Shakespeare, *Cymbeline*, act 4, scene 3.

[4]William Shakespeare, *Julius Caesar*, act 4, scene 3.

[5]Johann Wolfgang von Goethe, quoted in *John Lukacs, Remembered Past: John Lukacs on History, Historians and Historical Knowledge*, ed. Mark G. Malvasi and Jeffrey O. Nelson (Wilmington, DE: ISI Books, 2004), 5, 9.

[6]Jonathan Sacks, *Ceremony & Celebration* (New Milford, CT: Maggid Books, 2017), 215.

5. PROPHETIC UNTIMELINESS

[1]William Faulkner, *Requiem for a Nun* (New York: Vintage International, 1994), 73.

[2]H. Richard Niebuhr, *The Responsible Self: An Essay in Christian Moral Philosophy* (Louisville, KY: Westminster John Knox Press, 1999), 93.

[3]Niebuhr, *Responsible Self*, 93.

[4]Jonathan Sacks, *Covenant & Conversation—Exodus: The Book of Redemption* (New Milford, CT: Maggid Books, 2010), 93; George Santayana, *The Life of Reason*, vol. 1, *Reason in Common Sense* (New York: Scribner's, 1905), 284.

[5]Sacks, *Covenant & Conversation—Exodus*, 93.

[6]Sacks, *Covenant & Conversation—Exodus*, 93.

[7]Booker T. Washington, *Up From Slavery* (Tampa, FL: Millennium Publications, 2015), 70.

[8]Washington, *Up From Slavery*, 70.

[9]Hannah Arendt, *The Human Condition* (Chicago: University of Chicago Press, 1958), 233.

[10]Arendt, *Human Condition*, 244.

[11]Jonathan Sacks, *Haggada: Collected Essays on Pesach* (New Milford, CT: Maggid Books, 2013), 3.

[12]Much of the material in this section correlates closely with material in Os Guinness, *Impossible People: Christian Courage and the Struggle for the Soul of Civilization* (Downers Grove, IL: InterVarsity Press, 2016), 170-76, 179.

[13]Fyodor Dostoevsky, quoted in Henri du Lubac, *The Drama of Atheist Humanism* (San Francisco: Ignatius Press, 1995), 331.

[14]Richard Fisher, "The Perils of Short-termism: Civilization's Greatest Threat," *BBC*, January 10, 2019, www.bbc.com/future/story/20190109 -the-perils-of-short-termism-civilisations-greatest-threat.

[15]See G. K. Chesterton, "The Ethics of Elfland," in *Orthodoxy* (Garden City, NY: Image Books, 1959), chap. 4; and Jaroslav Pelikan, *The Vindication of Tradition* (New Haven, CT: Yale University Press, 1984), 65.

[16]Fisher, "Perils of Short-termism."

[17]Sacks, *Haggada*, 17.

[18]Jonathan Sacks, *Lessons in Leadership* (New Milford, CT: Maggid Books, 2015), 173.

[19]John Ralston Saul, *Voltaire's Bastards: The Dictatorship of Reason in the West* (New York: Simon & Schuster, 2013), 38.

[20]Anthony Storr, *The Essential Jung* (Princeton, NJ: Princeton University Press, 1983), 377.

[21]Reinhold Niebuhr, *Faith and History: A Comparison of Christian and Modern Views of History* (New York: Charles Scribner, 1949), viii.

[22]See Os Guinness, *The Last Christian on Earth* (Ventura, CA: Regal, 2010).

[23]George Tyrell, *Christianity at the Crossroads* (London: Allen & Unwin, 1963), 49.

[24]Peter L. Berger, *A Rumor of Angels* (New York: Penguin, 1963), 12; Peter L. Berger, *Facing up to Modernity* (New York: Basic Books, 1977), 163.

[25]John Ralston Saul, *Unconscious Civilization* (New York: Free Press, 1995), 19.

[26]Saul, *Unconscious Civilization*, 19.

[27]Friedrich Nietzsche, *Untimely Meditations*, trans. Anthony Ludovici (n.p.: Pantianos Classics, 1909), 148.

[28]C. S. Lewis, "Christian Apologetics," in *C. S. Lewis Essay Collection* (London: HarperCollins, 2002), 147.

[29]Lewis, "Christian Apologetics," 146.

6. THE END IS NOT THE END

[1]G. K. Chesterton, *The Everlasting Man*, G. K. Chesterton Collected Works 2 (San Francisco: Ignatius Press, 1986), 387.

[2]Reinhold Niebuhr, *Faith and History: A Comparison of Christian and Modern Views of History* (New York: Charles Scribner, 1949), 111.

[3]Niebuhr, *Faith and History*, 236.

[4]Jane Austen, *Persuasion* (London: Penguin Classics, 1998), 138; Søren Kierkegaard, *Journal* (Copenhagen: Søren Kierkegaard Research Centre, 1843), 18:306.

[5]Jonathan Sacks, *Covenant & Conversation—Genesis* (New Milford, CT: Maggid Books, 2009), 256.

CONCLUSION

[1]Friedrich Nietzsche, *The Birth of Tragedy*, in *The Philosophy of Nietzsche* (New York: Random House, 1927), 961.

[2]Sophocles, "Oedipus at Colonus," in *The Three Theban Plays*, trans. Robert Fagles (New York: Penguin, 1982), 358.

NAME INDEX

SUBJECT INDEX

ALSO BY THE AUTHOR

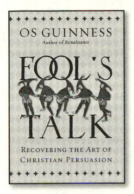

Fool's Talk
978-0-8308-4448-7

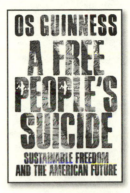

A Free People's Suicide
978-0-8308-3465-5

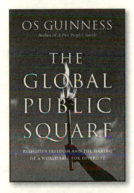

The Global Public Square
978-0-8308-3767-0

Renaissance
978-0-8308-3671-0

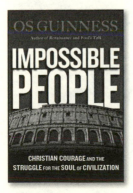

Impossible People
978-0-8308-4465-4

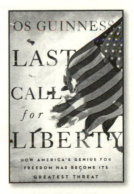

Last Call for Liberty
978-0-8308-4559-3